Taking Charge/
Managing Conflict

Taking Charge/
Managing Conflict

Joseph B. Stulberg

The Wooster Book Company

WOOSTER • OHIO

The Wooster Book Company
205 West Liberty Street
Wooster Ohio • 44691
www.woosterbook.com

ISBN 1-59098-147-2

Library of Congress Cataloging-in-Publication Data

Stulberg, Joseph B.
Taking charge / managing conflict.

Bibliography: p.
Includes index.
1. Conflict management. 2. Mediation. I. Title.
HD42.S78 1987
658.4—dc21   86.45597
                              CIP

In memory
of my mother and father,
and for
Jonathan, Michael, Gita, Charles, Heather,
and
Midge

Contents

Part III
The Lessons of Experience

Acknowledgments

M any of the examples that I use in this book are based on disputes in which I have served as a mediator. I want to acknowledge all those persons who permitted me to work with them in trying to achieve a settlement of their particular challenges. Others who have paved the way for me to serve as a mediator, or to enrich my understanding of the mediation process by training others to serve as mediators, include the original members of the Board of Directors of the Center for Dispute Settlement in Rochester, New York, Stanley Brezenoff, Michael L. Bridenback, Ronnie Brooks, Robert Coulson, Xenia Freeman, Lucy Friedman, J. Stanley Husid, Sanford Jaffe, Erwin J. Kelly, Gregory King, William F. Lincoln, Harold Newman, Mark Smith, Joanne Vilaghy, and, particularly, Christopher T. Whipple. By the power of their example, Earle C. Brown, the late Jack Kroner, and Sidney E. Pollick have influenced my style of dispute settlement intervention more than they could possibly know.

I have been stimulated to examine more closely many of the conceptual issues in this field of inquiry as a result of invigorating discussions with Robert A.B. Bush, Jane K. Cristal, Jack P. Etheridge, Margaret L. Shaw, and Frank E.A. Sander. My colleagues at Baruch College have provided me with a supportive environment in which to work; Richard Kopelman, Philip Ross, and Harris J. Shapiro were constant sources of encouragement. Almost every aspect of my thinking about matters in this area has been enriched by my treasured collaboration with J. Michael Keating, Jr.; he offered me his characteristically penetrating insights on every chapter of the penultimate draft and thereby saved me from making numerous mistakes.

In addition to my parents, two individuals indelibly shaped my intellectual development more than two decades ago: Elizabeth Giedeman, and, most especially, John Bruce Moore. In my experience, they remain scholars and pedagogues without peer; they showered me with their extraordinary talents and affection and, in so doing, immeasurably enriched the quality of my life. I feel privileged to be able to acknowledge publicly my enduring debt to them.

Bruce Katz, Susan Cummings, and their colleagues at Lexington Books have been inexhaustibly enthusiastic and supportive of my efforts to bring this work to fruition; that they could be so encouraging while simultaneously providing me with their probing assessments of the manuscript is a tribute to the professional manner in which they execute their responsibilities. Judy Ashkenaz did the copyediting, and Stephen Katigbak prepared the index.

Finally, and most important, I want to acknowledge my family for their constant support. Gita endured two summers at "Camp Dad," during which time I prepared the complete draft of the manuscript; I know that her tennis and swimming development did not suffer irreparably in the process, but her computer skills were put on hold as I systematically denied her access to our marvelous "Apple" machine. Sher Ilham eased my feelings of parental guilt by so lovingly nurturing Jonathan and Michael. Charles and Heather, in their inimitable way, kept themselves occupied while I finished the manuscript. My wife, Midge, helped to sustain this particular marathon effort through its many "walls" with her unwavering love and affection; I cannot envision engaging in this or any other of life's endeavors without her—nor would I want to.

To protect the reputations of all these wonderful people, I must make it clear that the use of names in the text is not intended to denote any actual persons, living or deceased, and that I alone am responsible for all the positions expressed and any errors contained herein.

1
Taking Charge

The scenes are familiar.

Employees threaten to strike for higher wages. College students disrupt classes to advocate U.S. resistance to apartheid in South Africa. Parents converge on a school board meeting to demand repeal of its decision to close their neighborhood school. Discussions become shouting matches. Tempers flare.

Suddenly, doors shut. Media personnel report that a mediator is meeting with the disputing parties. A statement is expected at the conclusion of their talks. Soon the parties emerge and announce that they have resolved their differences. Their controversy has evaporated into a settlement.

What happened? What did the mediator do that enabled those persons who had been entangled in controversy to resolve their differences?

Successful mediators are individuals skilled at forging a common ground among disputants. In a deliberate, conscious way, they force persons to clarify interests and transform rhetoric into proposals. They help disputants to develop settlement proposals that are tempered by political, legal, or resource constraints. They compel persons to establish priorities and consider trade-offs.

Mediators explore the significance of what is said and what is not said. They capitalize on inconsistencies and vulnerabilities to develop a framework for agreement.

Succinctly stated, mediators manage a dispute resolution process. Managing it effectively is no accident. Mediators develop particular skills, perform specific tasks, adhere to precise language practices, and deploy proven settlement-building strategies. These practices define the mediator's role. They can be identified and taught. Once learned, people can use them consciously and repeatedly when assisting others in resolving disputes.

All of us use mediation skills and strategies. Life demands them again and again. For example:

> Two independent divisions of a company market competing, non-compatible products to the same customer. The CEO dispatches a special assistant to meet with the two division presidents; his[a] job is to help them negotiate acceptable guidelines that sustain intracorporate independence and competition without unreasonably jeopardizing the continuing business relationship with valued customers.
>
> A parent interrupts his children's heated argument over what television program they will watch at 8:00 P.M. and assists them to discuss arrangements that each finds acceptable.
>
> A teacher gets two groups of shouting students to agree on how they will divide the use of the school's handball court during the lunch hour.
>
> Members of a community organization ask their most distinguished citizen to play peacemaker among the competing factions of the board of directors in order to minimize internal strife.

Conflict is inescapable. In some roles that we assume in our lives, we find ourselves intervening to help others resolve their disputes. That is what a mediator does. The question is not whether we will mediate. The only question is: How well will we do it?

---

[a] I have alternated the use of male and female gender by chapter in parts I and II. In chapter 12, I have alternated the use of male and female gender by question.

Part I
Concepts and
Principles of
Conflict Management

2

Intervenor Models

Mediation is a process whereby a neutral intervenor helps people involved in a dispute develop solutions that are acceptable to them. Unlike a judge or an arbitrator, the mediator has no authority to impose a binding decision on the disputants. He can only persuade them to settle.

There are many types of persuasive intervenors. A personnel director helps a supervisor and a subordinate resolve performance problems stemming from racial or ethnic bias. A city ombudsperson investigates citizen complaints against a public agency and seeks responses that will satisfy all concerned. A good samaritan breaks up a shouting match among teenagers in a public park and gets them to agree not to disturb each other.

But not all persuasive intervenors are mediators. Persuasive intervenors differ in the degree to which their role requires them to comply with and enforce independently established rules and standards. That degree of latitude determines the extent to which they can be neutral. Intervenors are neutral if they operate without any preference for resolving the controversy in one way rather than another. What distinguishes a mediator from other persuasive intervenors is his duty, both personally and institutionally, to be neutral.

When we compare persuasive intervenors' roles on the basis of the intervenor's duty to enforce independently established rules and standards, three distinct paradigms emerge: the intervenor as *compliance officer*, the intervenor as *manager*, and the intervenor as *developer*. These roles change as their freedom expands.

The Intervenor as Compliance Officer

Some intervenors help parties reach an agreement only if that agreement is compatible with corporate or institutional rules. If settlement terms violate those norms, then the intervenor must veto their consideration even if both parties find them acceptable.

Consider the trivial case of a corporate dress code. A subordinate refuses to wear white shirts as required. When his supervisor disciplines him, the subordinate appeals to an employee counselor to help them work out "a mutually satisfactory arrangement." The counselor can focus discussion on the propriety of the discipline but not on whether the rule is wise or desirable. He cannot permit the supervisor and the subordinate to make an exception to the rule even if the supervisor now asserts that he is agreeable to doing so. Even if the intervenor believes the rule is silly, he cannot join the quiet conspiracy to junk it. He must either change the rule through established procedures or change jobs.

The more rules there are, the less chance there is for the intervenor to be neutral in any meaningful sense. In disputes subject to a rule's application, one's responsibility as an intervenor is straightforward: persuade the people to comply with the governing rules.

The Intervenor as Manager

This type of intervenor helps disputants resolve their concerns in any way they find acceptable, even if the intervenor believes that their settlement terms are shortsighted, inefficient, or not in their best interests. There are two exceptions to this standard that the disputants' preferences are decisive, both tied to the legal system.

First, an intervenor does not allow parties to agree to settlement terms that are illegal. If a store owner fires an employee but later offers to rehire that person off the books so both can avoid paying taxes, the intervenor's duty as a citizen would prevent him from promoting such unlawful conduct even if the employee found it acceptable.

Second, an intervenor cannot require someone to discuss a matter over which that person has a legal right to act unilaterally. Suppose a company is considering relocating its manufacturing plant; town officials, concerned about the reduced tax base and lost employment opportunities that would result, ask a mediator to convene a meeting with them and company representatives to discuss the matter. Company personnel, for public relations or political reasons, might consent to attend such a meeting. But they don't have to meet; nor, if they meet, must they discuss the company's plans to relocate. Company officials are entitled to make this decision without joint participation. Despite town officials' heated pleas to expand the agenda, the intervenor as manager must eventually support the company's position, inform the others that the company is not legally compelled to negotiate such decisions, and bring the discussion—at least on that topic—to a close.

In practice, these two constraints are minimal. Most people don't parade their willingness to engage in illegal conduct before a mediator. In many contexts, establishing legal rights is irrelevant to the resolution of the conflict, or waiving a particular legal right is the most effective way for the parties to promote their overall interests.

Most persons discharge their mediating role in this posture of intervenor as manager. An adult watching children on a playground can help them resolve their argument over how long one group will use the ball field before relinquishing it to the other. An intervenor might persuade a landlord to waive his right to full payment of back rent in return for the tenant's commitment to pay some lesser amount in cash and vacate the premises promptly. Or an intervenor might help disputing stockholder factions develop an agreement for staging an agreed-on divestiture of its investments in companies doing business in South Africa. In each instance, the parties are free to design solutions they find acceptable; the intervenor's role is to facilitate that resolution process.

The Intervenor as Developer

Structured discussions with a persuasive intervenor can be an instrument for change. Customs, practices, laws, and values change over time. Individuals can prompt change as well as adjust to it.

The intervenor as developer assumes that no conventional rule is immutable and no topic ineligible for discussion. No mandatory standards exist for certifying the acceptability of settlement terms. This does not mean that everything is possible in a practical sense, but that reality represents an annoying practical problem rather than an impenetrable legal constraint.

Suppose a group of parents demand that school officials reduce the athletic budget and use the excess funds to purchase microcomputers for classroom use. The parents demonstrate in front of the high school to press their demand. Nothing would prevent an intervenor from having the school officials and protesting parents discuss this matter. Nothing need stop them from reaching an agreement, even if that agreement could not be implemented immediately because of existing contractual obligations with the teachers' union. All that the parties must acknowledge is that implementing their agreement requires additional collaboration with—and possibly amendment by—other constituencies.

This simple lesson bears repeating: practices and policies can be changed if people commit themselves to persevering through the discussion process. Advocating and securing change through discussion and persuasion is one of the principal nonviolent change-making procedures of a democratic society. Using a persuasive intervenor to direct such discussions can have a positive effect on developing the momentum and direction that enable such talks to succeed.

In such a context, there are no external standards restricting what one party must do. The intervenor is not required to support one party or another on any given issue. He is free to use whatever leverage he can obtain to influence parties to settle on terms they find acceptable.

Thus a *mediator* is a *neutral* intervenor. In terms of the three intervenor paradigms, the mediator operates as a manager or developer, not as a compliance officer. He enjoys enormous freedom in prodding disputants to consider a range of possible settlement terms. Although an indiviudal's own value system might lead him to refuse to serve in the role of mediator in certain disputes, as will be discussed later, a person must acknowledge that his power and effectiveness as a mediator emanate from his steadfast commitment to neutrality—to helping the parties develop settlement terms that *they* find acceptable, even if the mediator finds those terms objectionable.

It is easy to state that the parties' preferences should be decisive. It is much harder to act according to that precept. Most of us like to give orders to others. In our various roles as friends, co-workers, supervisors, parents, colleagues, group members, or citizens, we are always ready to dispense advice.

Mediating, however, demands that we shed our authoritarian and paternalistic instincts. It compels us to take seriously our commitment to democratic decision making, in our homes, schools, businesses, and communities. We pay a price for using such a process: people sometimes make mistakes, cater to greed, or act expediently. But to those who cherish freedom, the alternatives to mediated discussions are even less attractive.

Thus the challenge remains: How well will we mediate?

3
The Five P's of Conflict Management

W hat is a mediator getting herself into when she agrees to serve? Although the atmosphere differs in each dispute, there are patterns common to all controversies.

Perceptions

What is the first thing that comes to mind upon hearing the word *conflict*? Typical responses include:

anger
fear
tension
anxiety
frustration
distrust
hostility
damage
destruction
disruption

These responses reflect the negative connotation associated with the idea of a *dispute* or a *conflict*. Rarely do people associate disputes with such positive things as opportunities for personal growth, intellectual

---

The Five P's of Conflict Management

Perceptions:	Anger, fear, tensions, anxiety, etc.
Problems:	Disciplinary charges, noise, malpractice, divorce, etc.
Processes:	Give in, fight, litigate, mediate, etc.
Principles:	Efficiency, participation, justice, fairness, compliance, durability, etc.
Practices:	Power, self-interest, unique situations, combining processes

---

challenge, excitement, stimulation, or the like. Although the intensity of our feelings varies with the particular circumstances, most of us feel as though any dispute in which we are involved has only costs: emotional, financial, or social. We rarely perceive any benefits from being embroiled in a dispute. We consider a dispute to be an aberration from the more desirable state of harmony. If we were describing an ideal world, we would not include disputes as part of it.

This widespread way of thinking about disputes has a significant impact on how we approach resolving them. How do we resolve a situation that gives rise to anxiety, frustration, stress, or anger? *By eliminating the source of these negative feelings.* Anything short of that seems an undesirable compromise.

But acting on that impulse, though understandable, is utterly impractical. Suppose your neighbor's dog barks all night, making it impossible to sleep. A viable solution is not to shoot the dog or to make the neighbor move. If a ten-year-old disagrees with her parents about watching a violent movie on television, a viable solution is not for the child to leave home or for her parents to throw her out. An employee does not quit her job simply because a co-worker refuses to retract a stinging criticism. In such situations, some option other than elimination is needed.

Although eliminating the source of the controversy is impractical, the desire to do so is real. Some dispute resolution processes constrain that emotion more than others. Fighting permits an emotional and physical melee to develop, but fighting in a courtroom invites a contempt citation. Every mediator must appreciate the intensity of these antagonistic feelings and develop guidelines for addressing them. The challenge can be stated simply: How can the mediator reorient the way disputants see their problem so that they view a solution that does not involve the other's complete annihilation or capitulation as an acceptable, desirable outcome rather than a poor second choice?

Problems

What kinds of problems do we become entangled in? Think of conflicts that arise between persons or groups with the following relationships:

boyfriend–girlfriend
landlord–tenant
consumer–merchant
employer–employee
supervisor–subordinate
neighbor–neighbor
parent–child
sibling–sibling
spouse–spouse
doctor–patient
teacher–student
student–student
citizen group–government agency
minister–parishioners
agency staff–volunteers
developers–environmentalists
managers–ballplayers

prisoners–guards
agency personnel–service recipients
nation–nation

This list is not complete. It is sufficient, however, to reinforce several conclusions:

Disputes occur frequently, not just occasionally; they are part of everyday living.

Anyone can be involved in a dispute; disputes are not reserved for delinquents or fools.

Disputes differ; some are complicated or important, others simple or trivial.

The amount of time, money, and equipment needed for resolving a dispute will vary according to its complexity; peacekeeping efforts straitjacketed by spartan resources will never succeed.

Processes

Most of us resolve our disputes. How well we do so is another matter. But it is a myth—and a destructive one—to think that disputes are inherently unsolvable.

How do we actually resolve disputes? We might do one or more of the following:

give in
delay
avoid dealing with it
boycott
strike
create a task force to study the matter
consult an expert
litigate
vote

negotiate

mediate

arbitrate

legislate

bribe

fight or go to war

threaten

demonstrate

write a letter to the newspaper

appeal to the authority of our role (boss, parent) to decide the matter

lie or cheat

consult a friend or counselor

The list goes on. We are incredibly resourceful in finding ways to resolve disputes.

Just because we use these options at various times, however, does not mean we approve of all of them. The basis on which we select the process or combination of processes to use will be discussed later. First we must emphasize how mediation differs from the procedures we most frequently use.

We Americans tend to resolve disputes in one of four ways: fight, vote, litigate, or appeal to the authority of our role to render a decision. These methods share two essential characteristics: first, someone must win while the others lose; second, except in the case of fighting, it is assumed that everyone accepts the process and agrees to abide by its outcome, even if the result is contrary to everything she is trying to obtain. We assume, for instance, that losing parties in a lawsuit will comply with the judge's decision, that subordinates will implement their superiors' directives, that children will accept their parents' decisions as final, and that the losers of an election will abide by the election results. But we all know that life does not work so neatly.

Mediation differs from these methods on both of these fundamental points: it protects people from losing because each participant can veto a proposed solution, and it increases the probability that those involved will comply with the outcome by requiring those affected by the dispute to participate in developing solutions for it. Conceptually speaking, mediation is a dramatic departure from these standard processes because it makes us think strategically about how to persuade, not force, others to do what we want them to do. It requires us to treat people differently because we must convince others to cooperate with us in order to achieve our own goals. In practice, we use mediation techniques more frequently than we use these other procedures. Life demands it if we are simply to get from day to day.

Principles

A conscientious mediator operates with existential urgency. She must also act thoughtfully. Her efforts to help others are undermined to the degree that her analytical tools are blunted. Many questions bombard the mediator:

What does it mean for someone to compromise?

Must a mediator press parties to compromise in order for them to negotiate effectively?

Should a mediator attempt to get parties who do not trust one another to negotiate with each other?

In what sense is a mediator neutral?

What is power, and how can a mediator determine if there is a power imbalance among the parties?

What does it mean for a group to represent a broader constituency, and how does one know if the right representatives are involved in the mediated discussions?

How does one determine if a mediation effort has been successful?

These are not idle questions for the intellectually curious. Mediators must be ready to answer these questions in the heat of controversy. They are answerable, and they must be answered.

A more basic question arises, though. Consider the following:

Example 1. At the request of a group of irate parents, a mediator asks a school principal to meet with them to discuss their concerns about teacher disciplinary practices in the classroom. The principal refuses to do so, claiming that only the duly elected officers of the established Parent–Teacher Association, not the irate "troublemakers," should participate in such a discussion. How should a mediator respond?

Example 2. A police chief refuses to meet with a neighborhood association to negotiate its proposal to establish a citizen review board to monitor police conduct. She asserts that by agreeing to meet, she would establish an unfavorable precedent for resolving similar matters elsewhere and would undermine the mayor and city council members as the authorized representatives of, and spokespersons for, citizens concerned about public safety matters. Would a mediator requesting such a meeting have grounds for persuading the police chief to do otherwise?

These challenges force us to examine why we would choose to use mediation rather than some other process to resolve a given dispute. But that is only a particular instance of the fundamental question we must ask when resolving any dispute:

> *Why do we choose and prefer some processes for resolving certain disputes over others?*

On what basis, for example, do we choose to ignore rather than litigate a supervisor's denial of our request to take vacation time during August? Why don't we approve of letting high school students fight to resolve arguments that arise from relentless teasing or sexist name calling? Should we decide the location of toxic waste sites by public vote, legislation, or the operative forces of the private marketplace?

These are not easy questions. It is very important, however, that we all—practitioners and theoreticians alike—struggle with them. Each time we resolve a given dispute, we are choosing a particular dispute settlement process or combination of processes. In making that choice, we automatically give an answer—perhaps a controversial one—to this fundamental query.

We can answer the fundamental question in two steps. First, we must develop a set of standards for evaluating each dispute resolution process. Such standards include the following:

1. Efficiency (time and money) of the process from the participants' perspective

2. The public nature of the process

3. The degree and accuracy of fact-finding efforts necessary to support solutions

4. The precedents set by the results

5. The wisdom of the results

6. The degree of participation in the process of resolving the dispute by those who must live with the results

7. Compliance with and durability of the outcome

8. The fairness and justice of the process

9. The precedents set by using the process to resolve the particular dispute

10. The impact of using the dispute resolution process on the quality of the relationship among the disputing parties

11. The administrative costs of implementing the process

We then measure each process against these criteria. For example, *giving in* presumably consumes insignificant resources in terms of time and money, so it scores high on efficiency. But *giving in* certainly does not guarantee a wise solution to a conflict; hence the process scores low on that criterion.

After going through this empirical analysis for each process, we proceed to the second, and more difficult, step. We must now rank these criteria in the order of their importance. Doing that requires that we examine and apply the most fundamental principles of our individual and political morality: our right to freedom of thought and expression, our duty to treat others with equal respect and dignity, and the degree to which our liberty of action is justifiably constrained by considerations of fair play and integrity or is overridden by our interest in social order or economic growth. Once we decide which principle is most important to us in a given situation, we can determine which standard—efficiency, fairness, participation in the decision-making process, and so forth—shall be decisive. Then, drawing on the results of our empirical analysis in the first step, we choose the particular dispute resolution process.

Example 3. An employee believes that her corporation's accounting practices violate the law by impermissibly understating the extent of the company's future liability for paying pension benefits. Her supervisor, the vice-president in charge of finance, heatedly disputes the employee's analysis. How do they resolve this dispute? They may consult with other colleagues, or perhaps hire an outside consultant for her expert advice. But the employee typically does not go immediately to the monitoring government agency and "blow the whistle." First, she tries to resolve the dispute through internal channels. Why? Principles governing loyalty, affection, and responsibilities of individual group members toward one another compel her to choose a dispute resolution process—negotiation—that ranks high on the criterion of not irreparably damaging the continuing working relationship of the disputants.

Example 4. The decision to build a nuclear power plant affects many people. It also generates many disputes regarding location, size, and safety features, all of which dramatically affect the distribution of life's benefits and burdens among citizens and businesses alike. Our conception of a desirable political and economic community requires that we treat everyone with equal respect; that commitment prompts us to resolve these disputes in a way that ensures broad-based participation and open discussion, even at the expense of economic efficiency. Thus we choose to resolve controversies over such issues through the legislative and judicial processes rather than through private negotiation.

So we must restate the obvious. On the basis of a considered analysis of our fundamental values—moral, religious, political, economic, and aesthetic—we determine the priorities among those standards against which we will evaluate all dispute resolution processes. We then select a specific process for resolving a particular dispute in light of the empirical data that demonstrate how well that process operates according to the standards we have judged to be most important. Thus, each time we use a particular process to resolve a dispute, *no matter what the substantive outcome might be,* we make a statement about the values we cherish and the type of people we want to be.

Although every decision requires our making this normative commitment, the thought process described here is an ideal that we only approximate in practice. Time does not permit us to do otherwise. But there is no escaping the fact that we routinely make decisions that can only be justified by elaborating our reasoning according to this complex scheme. Simply consider the following:

Example 5. Community organizations stage a rally of three thousand protesters in front of a corporation that manufactures baby products. The protesters demand that the company immediately hire five hundred women and minority applicants within a thirty-day period and that the company cease all business activity in South Africa to protest that country's policy of apartheid. What factors does the company's president consider when deciding whether to meet with the protesters, ignore them, order the security guards to remove them from the grounds, initiate a public information campaign, or commence legal action to have the police remove the "trespassers" from the company's property? How do the company's commitments to generate profits, serve the community, and support such political rights as freedom of expression and association combine when the president makes her decision?

Example 6. Inmates at a state maximum-security prison take forty police guards as hostages and demand to negotiate with the governor of the state regarding living conditions, visitation arrangements, and educational programs at the prison. Should the governor agree to negotiate? Permit negotiations but only with her subordinates? Let the police treat the matter as a kidnapping and storm the prison with armed force? Create a special task force to study the matter and make recommendations? More important, on what basis would the governor

decide which options to pursue? What principles guide her
as she evaluates the competing claims of maintaining respect
for authority, protecting the hostages' lives and their families'
stake in their safety, preserving the prisoners' lives, protecting property, establishing a precedent for future situations,
promoting political advantages, protecting or ravaging the
personal reputation of individuals with official jurisdiction
over the prison system, and educating the public about the
events by providing for extensive media coverage?

How do these comments relate to mediators and the mediation
process? If we are to recommend the use of mediation to resolve a
dispute, we must do so by answering the fundamental question posed
here. Hence we must establish the strengths and weaknesses of mediation as a dispute resolution process by evaluating it according to the
standards noted previously and then identifying the broader values
and principles that support its choice.

Mediation requires the disputants to assume the major responsibility for resolving their conflict. Since all disputants must accept
the proposed solutions in order to reach agreement, it is counter-
productive for them to antagonize each other. Thus mediation does
not severely damage the parties' continuing relationship with one
another, and it deters unilateral attempts to skew the ground rules
in one side's favor or otherwise violate basic due process requirements.

The privacy of the mediated discussion promotes candid communication and deflates the public posturing that can intensify hostility. Further, mediation increases all parties' compliance with the outcome because people tend to abide by agreements achieved voluntarily.

Although the precedential value of the substantive agreement
reached through mediation is limited because its terms reflect only
the preferences and priorities of the particular parties involved, the
precedential value of using the mediation process to resolve certain
types of disputes is strong because its use acknowledges that all parties have concerns that must be addressed.

Mediation does not require parties to choose the best possible
solution or develop a strong factual underpinning to justify their
specific terms of agreement. Finally, although a mediated discussion

normally takes time to conclude successfully, and hence is not always efficient, its informal nature minimizes both administrative costs and the participants' direct financial costs.

Thus, mediation ranks at the lower end of the spectrum on the first five standards but fares very well on the remaining six.

To complete the second step of the analysis, we must identify those fundamental values that support our choice to use mediation rather than another dispute settlement process. The most fundamental principle, that of equality, requires us to treat each person with equal dignity and respect; mediation eliminates paternalism, authoritarianism, and bloodshed from dominating the decision-making process, and ensures that each decision maker counts as one and no more than one. We reinforce this principle through our commitment to democratic decision making: we believe that decisions should be made by the people, not by kings or technocrats, and mediation requires that those directly affected by the outcome participate in the decision-making process.

Our moral values emphasize the importance of individuals assuming personal responsibility for their conduct; mediation requires that individuals be held accountable for what they have done or plan to do. We cherish our membership in a social community; enjoyment of a rich, productive life is based on our interaction and interdependence with others, and successful mediation promotes community bonds by increasing communication and restoring trust among the disputing members. Finally, rather than blindly following some set of rules, we prefer to conduct ourselves according to the lessons of human experience; mediation supports this valued flexibility by permitting disputants to shape their own solutions to the problems they identify.

These principles constitute the core of the democratic way of life we treasure. They are constitutive of the mediation process. Mediation is not a radical process, but it is unusual in that it takes very seriously the rhetoric that all members of the community should be included as full participants in its various operations.

Practices

If mediation is so good, why don't people insist on using it all the time? Does it work in the real world and, if so, for what types of disputes? These questions will be answered in detail in later chapters.

Skeptics, however, offer four practical insights into why people "really" resolve disputes the way they do:

1. *Power:* If you have it, you can hide or rationalize your decision by using any process you choose. If you don't have it, you must dance to the other's tune.

2. *Self-interest:* People choose the dispute resolution process that they believe will enable them to prevail. Any talk about respect, dignity, and participation in the process is nonsense. People act to further their self-interest. If someone expects to win a lawsuit, she will sue; if she thinks she might lose, she will consider other options.

3. *Unique situations:* Every situation is different. It is foolish to believe that one should always prefer mediation to other dispute settlement procedures, or that one can know in advance which process might be best.

4. *Combining processes:* A savvy person does not put all her eggs in one basket. Rather than rely exclusively on mediation, she might use a combination of dispute settlement processes to resolve a dispute.

The skeptics warn us not to be naive about these elements of human behavior when trying to resolve disputes. But they overstate their case. We must analyze their concerns here in order to prevent them from plaguing our subsequent discussion.

Power. It is true that people who have the unilateral power to get what they want have no need for mediation. Indeed, they have no need for anyone; they should simply do whatever they must in order to achieve their goals. But it is extremely rare that anyone has this much one-sided power. Abused children can get police assistance. Corporate presidents need shareholder approval and subordinate cooperation to achieve their stated objectives. And the list goes on.

No one denies that in particular circumstances, some individuals have more power than others. A boss often has more power than her subordinate over the latter's continued employment status; the young woman living in the upstairs apartment has the power to disrupt her downstairs neighbor's peace and quiet by playing drums at 2:00 A.M.;

and the teacher has the power to affect a student's academic success. But the skeptics jump from acknowledging those realities to concluding that the victim has *no* power. That's just not so. Some people may act as though they are both infallible and invincible, but we are all vulnerable in some ways. In appropriate circumstances, the employee can challenge her boss by filing a grievance, speaking to a superior, or starting a lawsuit. The apartment dweller can complain constantly to the landlord. The student can spread damaging rumors about the teacher. Whether people recognize that they have power—or, more important, have the desire and courage to use it—are separate considerations that have very practical consequences. Few of us, however, are completely powerless all the time.

Self-Interest. The insight that people and groups choose processes that promote their self-interest is meaningless until we define *self-interest*. Once we do so, the "insight" is useless.

Suppose, for example, that a tenant has fallen behind in her rent payments by two months. When the landlord asks her about it, the tenant reminds her of an earlier conversation in which the tenant informed the landlord that her kitchen appliances were not working and that she would not pay any rent for as long as that condition persisted. The landlord decides to consult you. She defines her self-interest as "getting as much money as possible from the tenant" and asks for advice about which dispute resolution process to use. What would you advise? You would not say "Do whatever promotes your self-interest"—that would leave the landlord with no better idea of what to do than before she asked you for help. But you *could* help her by identifying the possible outcomes of using competing dispute resolution processes, thereby forcing her to define her "self-interest" more sharply.

For instance, you might point out that she would win the largest monetary award by suing her tenant, but she would have to reduce that award by at least the amount of money spent on attorneys' fees, the cost of advertising for a new tenant, and any rent money lost by having a vacant apartment for any period of time. An alternative would be to engage promptly in mediated discussions and press for a settlement that minimally recoups some of the rent arrears in return for her promptly fixing the appliances.

What does the landlord mean by "getting as much money as possible from the tenant"—getting the highest total dollar amount from the tenant regardless of the costs incurred to obtain it, or getting the highest *net* amount from the tenant? The landlord must assess the strengths and weaknesses of each possible dispute resolution process in order to identify her preferred outcomes or components of self-interest; then she can choose to use the procedure most likely to secure them.

If the skeptic retorts, "Just as I said, in the end she simply chooses the process that will promote her self-interest," the response is twofold. First, now we know what the person means by self-interest, whereas previously it was a vacuous idea. Second, the skeptic is confusing what motivates a person to choose one process with the obligations the person assumes as a participant in it. *Motives* for acting are not identical with *reasons* for acting. My motivation for selecting the arbitration process might be to promote my self-interest; I may believe I have a sure-fire case, prefer the privacy of the arbitration process to a public trial, and want the matter resolved definitively as quickly as possible. By agreeing to arbitration, however, I agree to submit my case to the arbitrator and let her render a final and binding decision. I make the most persuasive presentation I can marshal that is consistent with the rules of the arbitration process. If the arbitrator decides against me, however, I cannot then choose not to comply with her decision because doing so would be contrary to my previously defined self-interest; by agreeing to arbitration, I made certain commitments to interact with others according to certain guidelines, to which they can now hold me accountable.

In the real world, of course, people do violate their obligations in just such circumstances—they lose and then want to change the rules of the game. But we can anticipate that possibility and take steps to minimize its occurrence.

Unique Situation. Though each dispute is different, we do develop steady patterns of behavior. It is silly to deny that disputes and disputants have similarities. Next-door neighbors, for example, often become embroiled in disputes over the use of a common driveway. It is not unreasonable to presume that their problems can be handled by using the same dispute resolution process and, perhaps, can even be resolved in comparable ways. The danger that the skeptics correctly point out is that of converting the presumption of similarity into an immutable truth. The challenge, then, is to identify those ways in which disputes or disputants differ from one another that would justify our treating them differently. If we use due process hearing procedures to review disciplinary actions taken against high school students, for example, should we apply the same procedure when elementary school students are involved? These questions force us to reconsider those fundamental values that guide our selection of one dispute settlement process over another. This "insight" sheds no light; it simply restates our starting point.

Combining Processes. The skeptics note, correctly, that people often use several dispute resolution processes simultaneously. Those who oppose the construction of a new federal highway might attempt to block its development by initiating court action, while simultaneously conducting a sit-in at the proposed site, picketing city hall, and offering to participate in professionally mediated discussions with various government officials and private developers to try to reach a resolution. Lawyers often initiate a lawsuit on behalf of their clients but then negotiate a settlement "on the courthouse steps" just before the trial.

But the skeptics have paid less attention to the way in which using one process can distort or undermine the use of others. Let's consider an obvious foul-up: state officials agree to meet at 3:00 P.M. with a group of prisoners who are holding prison guards as hostages; simultaneously, they order state police officers to storm the prison beginning at 3:00 P.M., using whatever force is necessary to quash the uprising. Although some might applaud the use of the negotiating session as a decoy, clearly both processes cannot genuinely operate at the same time. Other examples indicate that we can operate at cross-purposes in far more subtle ways.

Suppose two people decide to divorce; they have two children, ages five and seven. How should they settle their differences with respect to dividing their property, caring for the children, and assuming financial obligations? If one party, say the wife, initiates a lawsuit, the other party must respond or jeopardize his legal posture. Assume the wife, or her lawyer, then suggests to the husband, or his lawyer, that they try to negotiate a settlement. But a new dynamic has now entered the negotiation process. The husband is a party to a lawsuit. He may be cautious about considering any settlement option that might force him to share information that could be damaging in subsequent litigation.

The continued posturing that accompanies the assertion of legal rights escalates the tension and bitterness among the disputants, thereby undermining the constructive future relationship that the negotiation process, when operating alone, is designed to promote. By placing the negotiations within the framework of a lawsuit, one immediately undermines the problem-solving spirit so essential to effective negotiations. Getting an agreement in such circumstances is not impossible, but it is normally more difficult. The dynamic among the parties would be significantly different if they committed themselves to trying to resolve their differences through joint discussions for a specified time period and initiating litigation only if such efforts failed.

We operate in a complex world. No dispute resolution process operates in a vacuum. We often use several processes simultaneously in order to signal to others that we are serious about our aspirations and expect to be treated accordingly. Having acknowledged that, however, we must make certain the strategy does not backfire. We must ensure that simultaneous use does not diminish the processes' distinctive strengths.

Mediation is not a panacea, but it is a remarkably effective process for resolving a wide range of controversies—from those among co-workers or quarreling siblings to those among nations trying to secure the peaceable exchange of political prisoners.

Successful mediation is not an accident. A mediator does more than just "stay loose" or "use common sense." She acts in deliberate, thoughtful, and structured ways to try to bring about settlements. No mediator can ever guarantee a successful outcome, but she will not stop trying to create one until she has exhausted every available strategy. In part II we examine the elements of successful mediation efforts.

Part II
Mediation Skills
and Strategies

4

The Mediator's Job

The mediator's job is to get negotiating parties to agree to terms that resolve their dispute. We must identify the specific responsibilities that define his job and those personal qualities that enable him to execute his tasks.

Job Description of a Mediator

The mediator has primary responsibility for structuring and managing discussions directed at achieving mutually acceptable solutions to the issues in dispute. His specific functions are both procedural and substantive.

Chairperson

The mediator is responsible for scheduling the number, time, and place of meetings. He establishes the format of each meeting and the number of persons who participate. He arranges for making typing, photocopying, telephone, and other support services available for the parties. Substantively, he is responsible for focusing the discussion and maintaining control over the parties' behavior. A mediator performs this function in every dispute, although the extent to which it applies varies with the situation.

> *Example.* A teacher who tries to resolve a dispute between two students who are throwing food at each other in a school cafeteria does not have to worry about scheduling meetings or providing clerical services to the disputants. Yet he must chair or direct the discussions among them. He must create

some format or environment in which they can effectively deal with each other rather than let them stand at opposite ends of the room and shout at each other in front of a hundred other students.

A person who mediates a dispute between a landlord and a tenant organization while a rent strike is in progress must consider such issues as where to meet, who should be present, and the scheduling of multiple meetings.

Communicator

Parties to a dispute often do not understand what others are saying. The mediator must transmit ideas, positions, convictions, and emotions among them in such a way that they understand each other. Mediators must also realize that people frequently communicate indirectly.

> *Example.* Smith vehemently accuses his neighbor, Jones, of kicking him in the shins, but then focuses the rest of his discussion on his concern that Jones's dog comes onto his property, kicks over his garbage can, and scatters the garbage all over the yard. Smith has communicated some very important information—namely, that his concern about the alleged assault and battery pales in significance next to his desire to control the dog's behavior. The mediator must make certain that Jones understands those priorities so that discussion is appropriately focused.

Educator

The mediator must empathize with the aspirations of the respective parties and understand the technical aspects of each substantive proposal. He must then be able to convey that information effectively to those who lack that knowledge. The stakes are higher than in conducting a mere classroom exercise; a mediator must persuade parties to act on the basis of their understanding.

> *Example.* A mediator cannot say: "I don't know how else to explain to you the school district's discussion of the financial

ramifications of your proposal to keep the neighborhood school open on weekends so that your children can use its facilities." He *must* find an effective way to explain such matters as liability and property insurance coverage, custodial costs, and pertinent contractual obligations with the affected unions. Otherwise, he assumes the risk of not getting an agreement simply because one party does not understand the constraints under which the other is operating.

Translator

Parties sometimes fail to reach agreement not because what is said is objectionable but because the language in which the proposal is couched triggers hesitation, fear, or some other negative response. The mediator's function is to translate statements or proposals into language that increases their probability of being favorably received. The mediator never camouflages or eliminates portions of a proposal when translating; his task is to reduce the sting of its language.

> *Example.* When talking with management, a mediator translates a union's proposal for a $4.50/hour wage increase into a wage offer of 7 percent. The mediator translates a neighbor's proposal that the seventeen-year old not play his record player from 11:00 P.M. until 7:00 A.M. each night into an offer to the teenager that enables him to play his record player seven days a week from 7:00 A.M. until 11:00 P.M.—sixteen hours a day!

Resource Expander

A mediator must increase the range of resources that parties use to resolve their dispute. He can do this by generating additional information that is germane to the controversy, suggesting new ideas for settlement, setting up meetings between the parties and particular individuals to whom they had previously lacked access, and leveraging other services that can help the parties resolve their concerns.

> *Example.* A mediator might help a parent and his teenage child resolve some of their problems by identifying some pertinent

counseling services or planned recreational programs that they
can then agree to investigate using for a specified time period.

Agent of Reality

The mediator must be able to identify for each party what is do-able
in light of the interests and resources of the other parties to the discussion. If a party's proposal is inflated, the mediator must let him know
that it is simply unobtainable.

> *Example.* The parent group of the neighborhood elementary
> school is concerned about the extremely low scores their
> children received on a standardized reading test. They blame
> the school principal for this dismal state of affairs and demand to meet with the school superintendent for the express
> purpose of insisting that he fire the principal as an indication of his commitment to correcting the situation. The superintendent adamantly refuses to meet under such conditions,
> but does offer to meet with the parents and the principal to
> discuss the school's reading program; the parents then refuse
> to meet. A mediator, after canvassing the situation, must indicate strongly to the parents that their demand to have the principal fired simply will not be met. If they want to talk to the
> superintendent or other school officials about improving their
> children's reading skills, they must first drop this demand as
> a condition for meeting, if not drop it altogether. The mediator
> does this not because he believes the superintendent is correct and the parents are wrong; he does it on the basis of his
> assessment that the superintendent will not change his position and that the parents must modify their demands if they
> want to have any discussions at all.

Guardian of Durable Solutions

The mediator should not impose on the parties his own judgment
or preference as to how a problem should be resolved. But the mediator
must consider the consequences of what people are agreeing to and
try to ensure that the terms of agreement they develop will last.

Example. Out of impatience to conclude the discussion, parties sometimes agree to do things that are not practical. Neighbors, for example, might agree to stop the periodic fighting between their nine-year old children by forbidding them ever to play with each other again; but if the children are classmates in school, the agreement will not be honored. A tenant might agree to move out of his apartment in one week; but if there are no vacant apartments in the area that he can afford, the tenant won't budge. While remaining neutral, the mediator must try to prevent the parties from agreeing to solutions that will not work in practice.

Scapegoat

The mediator is the lightning rod for the parties' frustrations and concerns. He is the blamepost on which parties hang their excuses.

Example. Parties want to express their frustration and anger at the obstructiveness and obstinacy of their adversaries. If they directly accuse each other of such behavior, however, they increase their mutual antagonism and jeopardize any potential agreement. What do the parties do instead? They loudly blame the mediator for being ineffectual. This enables them to communciate their frustration and growing impatience to each other without risking an immediate breakdown in discussions.

Similarly, negotiators can tell their constituents: "We don't like the settlement, but the mediator claims this is all any of us can possibly obtain in these talks, and he refuses to schedule any more discussions, so it was this or nothing." This face-saving device of blaming the mediator for the settlement terms serves several purposes: it enables the negotiators to continue to advocate their group's demands while modifying the group's position in order to reach an agreement. It also allows them to accept terms of settlement without having to acknowledge publicly that they have caved in to the other's demands.

Protector of the Process

The mediator is responsible for protecting the integrity of the mediation process. This process is a useful vehicle for helping parties resolve disputes. Sometimes, however, a party has no genuine interest in talking with others about what he is doing or planning to do, but is merely using the mediator and the process as a tactical decoy to help him achieve his end. The mediator must promptly quash any such effort.

> *Example.* A commercial developer agrees to participate in mediated discussions with a group of citizens who are concerned about his plans to build a fish hatchery in their small seaside resort town. By agreeing to meet, he generates the expectation within the citizens' group that its concerns about plant size, environmental impact, and increased traffic over local roads will be openly discussed and resolved collaboratively. If the developer then refuses to provide requested information, periodically misses scheduled meetings, requests postponements because of "unexpected emergencies," and refuses to consider the strengths or weaknesses of any proposals but his own while simultaneously proceeding quietly to obtain the necessary authorization and permits to build the plant exactly as he wishes, then he is using the legitimacy of the process and the aura of "good-faith mediated discussions" to dupe his adversaries. The mediator cannot allow any party to subvert the process in this way.

These nine responsibilities constitute the mediator's job. They make his presence a valued one, although they certainly are not designed to help him win a popularity contest. That is as it should be; the parties must live with the agreement, not with the mediator. The mediator is a catalyst. His presence makes a difference. His participation automatically affects the dynamics of how disputants interact with one another. A mediator cannot be frivolous in executing his tasks; an inept performance can antagonize parties, increase tension, and shatter the possibility for agreement. It is nonsense to assert that since only the parties can accept terms of settlement, it does not matter whether the mediator performs his tasks well or haphazardly;

he must perform his job conscientiously and constructively if they are to reach acceptable terms of settlement.

We now examine those personal characteristics and abilities that enable people to execute these functions capably.

Job Qualifications of a Mediator

What kind of person is a mediator? Is he the proverbial nice guy who finished last and decided to try peacekeeping for a living? Is he a demanding, aggressive, high achiever or a passive, quiet individual?

To determine the personal qualities and abilities an effective mediator needs, adopt the perspective of a party to a dispute and answer this question: If a mediator were to assist you in your discussions with the other parties, what characteristics and skills would you want him to possess? Your list would look something like this:

1. *Neutral.* A mediator must have no personal preference that the dispute be resolved in one way rather than another. He is there to help parties identify solutions that they find acceptable, not simply to gang up on one of the participants. Every disputant, naturally, would prefer to have a mediator who always supports his viewpoint. But since a mediator cannot do that for everyone, each party wants someone who at least is not working against him. If a mediator is not neutral, then there is no reason for the disputants to trust him.

2. *Impartial.* A mediator must treat all parties in comparable ways, both procedurally and substantively. Justice requires it and effectiveness demands it. He cannot address some persons informally but others by title, convene meetings at sites that are inconvenient to some but advantageous to others, or encourage parties to consider settlement terms from which the mediator would personally profit.

3. *Objective.* A mediator must be able to transcend the rhetoric and emotion of the parties. He must analyze proposed solutions with detachment in order to assess their strengths and weaknesses accurately and build his settlement strategy accordingly.

4. *Intelligent.* Parties are looking to the mediator for assistance. Although parties must educate the mediator about the specific problem, they do not want to be handicapped by a mediator's general slowness of mind.

5. *Flexible.* A mediator must promote, not retard, the fluidity of the discussions. If a party makes a casual remark indicating a change

of position on an issue but the mediator refuses to discuss it until the current agenda item is resolved, the mediator's rigidity becomes the source of the impasse. The mediator must manage the process and chair the discussions, but he must not wear blinders while doing so.

6. *Articulate.* A mediator must be verbally astute in order to communicate a thought, perspective, or proposal of one party to another. A mediator must choose his words wisely and speak concisely. People grow weary of listening to mediators who cannot state matters clearly and intelligibly, who do not complete their sentences or who end each statement with "and, uh. . . ."

7. *Forceful and persuasive.* A mediator must be forceful enough to convince disputants to be reasonable and flexible. Parties do not want a mediator who merely accepts on faith the respective claims of the various disputants and then exhorts them to find a way to resolve their difficulties.

8. *Empathetic.* A mediator must be able to appreciate the thoughts, fears, history, and perceptions that lace together each party's proposals. Parties don't need someone to tell them to love one another. They want help in resolving their practical concerns in the real world of power, rights, obligations, and possibilities—not in some utopia. The mediator's capacity for empathy gives them confidence that the alternative solutions they are exploring with the mediator will not ignore their needs.

9. *Effective as a listener.* A mediator must hear and comprehend the concerns of all parties. If a mediator is constantly talking or asking questions, the parties will not believe he is interested in understanding their problems as *they* see them. A mediator, above all, must appreciate the wisdom of the saying "It is no accident that people are made with two ears and one mouth."

10. *Imaginative.* If a mediator cannot offer fresh ideas or different perspectives on the problem, his presence adds nothing of value to the discussion. One need not be a genius to be imaginative. One way to resolve a dispute between siblings who are fighting over which television show to watch at 8:00 P.M. is to suggest that they hook up the video cassette recorder to the television set and record one show while they watch the other. Kids (and grown-ups, too) can get so wrapped up in arguing over trivial matters (who watched his program first last week, or who turned the TV on) that they overlook some obvious solutions.

11. *Respected in the community.* A mediator does not need to be famous, but he must be a capable individual whose presence, at the very least, does not constitute an insult to the parties. Everyone believes his own problems are important, and they are. Disputants want a mediator whose background or reputation lends stature to their discussions. Disputants feel confident that their concerns are being accorded respect if the chairperson of the town's biggest employer serves as mediator; conversely, suggesting that a street bum mediate their dispute is derogatory and demeaning to the parties, not to mention useless.

12. *Skeptical.* The mediator should not diminish the credibility of the process by exploring proposals that are impossible or outrageous. Parties want an accurate reading of each other—what they want and what they are willing to live with. The mediator cannot be so gullible as to believe that he should make parties consider *every* suggestion or offer that is made; doing that simply transforms him into a mere puppet of the disputing parties. The mediator serves the parties well by eliminating fruitless discussions, even if that results in failure to reach a negotiated agreement.

13. *Able to gain access to resources.* A mediator must have sufficient stature and power to gain access to those resources that are necessary or helpful for resolving the dispute. The parties might need to convey their concerns to the company president, mayor, governor, school superintendent, or some other official with significant power to influence the outcome. If the parties themselves do not have access to such resources, the mediator must fill the gap.

14. *Honest.* The mediator's integrity must be beyond reproach. Since the parties don't always trust each other, they must be able to trust the mediator. No one will trust someone who misleads or deceives him.

15. *Reliable.* If the mediator says he will do something—gather certain information, contact particular individuals, or prepare a draft of the agreement—he had better do it. Parties do not need a mediator who always has an excuse for failing to deliver.

16. *Nondefensive.* A mediator must be able to absorb a party's venting its frustration and criticism of the process or of the mediator himself. He need not apologize for his efforts if he has done the best he can, but he must be able to know when to absorb the abuse and

blame without comment and when to confront it. For the most part, a mediator has to stifle his reactions, for he does not always know what is behind the outburst.

17. *Having a sense of humor.* A mediator must be able to laugh, both with others and at himself. The deft use of humor can relax tensions, put people at ease, or make a point in a subtle way. No mediator should make an individual party the object of ridicule or the butt of his one-liners, nor should his humorous remarks be at the expense of particular groups or classes of people. But the mediator should not make the mistake of believing that serious business cannot be conducted with some laughter.

18. *Patient.* Every mediator knows that the shortest route to a settlement is not a straight one. A mediator must be prepared to manage the discussion through all the side streets that lead eventually to that destination. Parties want someone who will assist them no matter how long it takes. They don't want a mediator to tell them that their matter must be resolved in twenty minutes because he has to leave for a business meeting or tennis date. They don't want a mediator who acts like a stereotypical bureaucrat who simply processes their dispute along with hundreds of others. They want to be heard. They want to express their concerns in their own language. They want to tell the mediator what they believe is relevant to their dispute, rather than being restricted to responding to questions on a form. All this takes time, and no one's patience is inexhaustible, but the mediator should be the last person to lose it. The mediator's rule of thumb is that it takes the first 90 percent of the total discussion time to resolve 10 percent of the issues and the final 10 percent of the time to solve the remaining 90 percent. The lesson is clear: the mediator can't force a settlement down the parties' throats; he must be prepared to take the time to listen to their concerns and move the disputants toward agreement at a measured pace.

19. *Persevering.* The mediator must be able to persevere. Not naively, of course—not if there is no sign of progress. But every discussion, whether it lasts three minutes or three months, proceeds by spits and spurts, starts and stutters. Disputants become exasperated when it seems that they take three steps backward for every two steps forward. Even when agreement appears within their grasp, something can happen to set back the prospect for resolution. The mediator

cannot quit. He must get past the exasperation born of fatigue and continue to press the parties to clarify details or reexamine the strengths and weaknesses of proposals. He must be prepared to go the distance without really knowing how far that is.

20. *Optimistic.* A mediator must be upbeat. He must charge the discussions with an electricity that gives people confidence that they can resolve their concerns. He must inspire them to believe in their ability to shape their own future. Consider a mountain climber who must cross a crevasse in order to survive. Will he make it? The objective facts are not encouraging: a greater-than-normal distance, heavy boots, inclement weather. But these "facts" ignore the climber's will to believe he can make it. Surely, the success of his leap will be affected by his belief that he will or will not succeed. A mediator must provide this positive element to the dispute settlement discussions.

But a mediator does not serve the parties well if he is a naive optimist or a pollyanna. He must be realistic and candid with all parties about the likelihood of success. Still, the mediator should not confuse being realistic with being an automatic nay-sayer. Nothing is more discouraging to disputants than always to be told why something *can't* be done. Most people dislike the idea of being involved in a dispute; they want it resolved, and they don't need someone to reinforce their misery by reminding them of the hopelessness of their situation.

These are the characteristics and abilities that parties to a dispute want to see in their mediator. Obviously, none of us has all of these qualities in abundance. But we do possess them in sufficient, though varying, degrees to enable us to execute the mediator's role effectively.

Now we know what the mediator's job involves and the qualifications for it. We can't decide not to apply for the job—life won't let us. So, humbled but excited by the challenge, we proceed. How do we get started?

5
Assess Your Point of Entry

A mediator does not operate in a vacuum. She joins conflicts in progress and helps the disputants to manage their subsequent discussions. The mediator must not begin by stepping on mines. She must scout the terrain. She must identify the players. She must determine if mediation is appropriate. She must decide whether her presence would be constructive.

PRIOR-TO Mediating: Anatomy of a Conflict

Although every dispute differs significantly in its details, all disputes have an identical structural framework, which consists of the following seven components: parties (P); resources (R); issues (I); options of the dispute resolution forum (O); rules affecting behavior (R); time constraints for resolution (T); and outcomes (O)—PRIOR-TO, for short. The mediator's first task is to apply this framework to the particular situation at hand. She must answer the question: What has happened PRIOR-TO her appearing on the scene? Gathering the information to answer this question, however, requires a clear understanding of the elements that make up these essential components of a dispute.

Parties

A mediator must distinguish between those persons who are involved in the dispute and those who are both involved in it and shall be *parties* to the discussion. Every dispute involves people who are identifiable to and by one another. Disputants can have various types of relationships to one another; they can participate in mediated discussions

---

PRIOR-TO Entry:
Examining the Structural
Components of a Dispute

Parties:	Persons known to each other who advocate distinct, clashing positions on a given matter and have the apparent power to frustrate each other's actions or satisfy each other's concerns
Resources:	People, information, finances, and publicity to which parties and mediator have recourse
Issues:	Matters, practices, or actions that enhance, alter, frustrate, or in some way adversely affect some person's interests, goals, or needs
Options of forum:	Dispute resolution processes that are available to the parties
Rules affecting behavior:	Laws, institutional rules, professional codes of conduct, industry practices, and social conventions that establish range of possible settlement options
Time frame:	Deadlines within which outcomes must be developed
Outcomes:	Dispositions of issues, varying in form, type, and specificity

---

as individuals, groups, corporations, or governments. (A company that loses a substantial amount of its property to *unknown* individuals does not have a *dispute* with those perpetrators; it does, however, have a serious *problem* of vandalism, for which a strategic plan of action must be developed.)

Identifying which people are both *involved* in the dispute and must be *parties* to its resolution is often easy. Two neighbors have no difficulty identifying their two ten-year old sons as the only persons involved in a dispute over who will play pitcher first and who will be at bat. Similarly, for disputes among divorcing couples, landlords and tenants, supervisors and subordinates, homeowners and contractors, and professors and students, the parties to the dispute are easily identifiable. But some disputes are more complex, and distinguishing the parties to the dispute from the people involved in it can be considerably more difficult.

Suppose a homeowner wants to operate a day care facility out of her home. She applies to a governmental agency for approval. Some neighborhood residents want to prevent this development from occurring, other neighbors actively support it, and some don't care. Are all these persons involved in this dispute—and, if so, in what ways?

The dispute here appears to be between the homeowner who wants to operate the facility and those neighbors who oppose it. They would be *parties* to the mediated discussions since they have distinct, clashing positions on the matter, with the apparent power to frustrate each other's actions or satisfy each other's concerns.

What about the government official and the other neighbors? They are *involved* in the dispute, but should they be *parties* to the mediated discussions? If the government official operates under a policy mandate to establish as many residential day care facilities as possible, then she has a distinct interest in how this dispute is resolved; she is a party to the dispute and would assume a separate spot at the discussion table. But if the policy is simply to grant approval to all such proposals as long as they comply with statutory guidelines, then, although she is involved in the dispute in the sense that operating the facility requires her official authorization, she is indifferent to whether the neighbors agree to let it operate or not; she is not a party to the dispute.

All the other neighbors can also be said to be *involved* in the dispute in the sense that their daily activities will be affected by the outcome; if the facility is approved, for example, they might have to drive more carefully down the street at certain times of day. Indeed, one might claim that the entire community is involved, for in a limited sense all the following people are affected by the decision: the parents of the children who would use the facility; the local employers who experience increased absenteeism or low productivity when their employees must struggle to find adequate day care facilities for their young children; the children who would attend the facility; the workers who would be employed at it; the businesses that would prosper by virtue of increased purchases of supplies by this project; and all the taxpayers who might pay less in the future for special school programs, social services, or law enforcement activities if high-quality care were made available to people at an early age.

Should all these individuals be parties to the discussions? To answer this requires us to apply those fundamental principles of individual and political morality that structure all our choices of a dispute resolution process. If we believe that decisions involving the location of day care centers should be made by anyone who is affected in any way, then the mechanism used must be one, such as voting, that enables everyone to express her preference. If, however, we prefer to have the matter resolved by those who perceive their interests to be most significantly affected by the proposed action, then the number of *parties* to the discussions is dramatically smaller than the number of persons affected by the ultimate decision.

In controversies like this one, we encourage those who are most tangibly affected by the matter to work out a satisfactory solution among themselves. There is no ready formula to answer the question: Who should be involved in the discussions? In the matter just described, two parties to the dispute seem obvious. But what if a citywide organization of "Parents for Day Care Facilities" took an active interest in supporting this application? Should its role be that of "concerned bystander," of a "constituent" who is "represented" by the person trying to establish the facility, or of a group with a distinct interest in the outcome that merits its taking a principal role in the discussions?

The challenge is clear: the mediator must identify the people who will participate in the discussions. Some suggestions for meeting that challenge appear in the next section.

Resources

Each party to a dispute possesses certain resources: people, information, money, and access to others such as politicians or the news media.

A mediator likewise has resources: time, experience, reputation, access to others, and support services. Levels of available resources have a dramatic effect both on the way discussions take place and on their outcome. Power relationships among the participants, for instance, vary according to their available resources and affect the range of probable settlement options; similarly, a mediator who is systematically deprived of essential information by the parties will be ineffective in developing leverage points for moving the parties toward agreement.

Issues

Issues are those matters, practices, or actions that enhance, frustrate, alter, or in some way adversely affect some person's interests, goals, or needs. Resolving a dispute means solving its issues.

Issues are distinct entities. They differ from facts, assumptions, principles, and problems. The mediator's role in helping parties identify issues clearly and thoroughly may be her most important contribution to the dispute settlement process. Think of how often a parent effectively stops a shouting match between her children simply by helping them to understand clearly exactly what they were shouting about.

Options of Dispute Resolution Forum

Practically speaking, the range of available process options for resolving a dispute depends on the people, resources, and issues involved. Four students who are arguing over who gets to use the school playground's handball court first will not sue each other to resolve the issue. But citizens protesting the construction of a high-voltage transmission line that will cross their property might initiate court action, seek protection from the legislature and the governor, and picket the offices of the utility company that proposes to construct the line.

Some people have a developed tradition or practice for resolving disputes. Some families have weekly family meetings where individual members can voice their complaints about events that have occurred during the week (such as household assignments). Unions and management bargain over such matters as wages and hours of employment; they know that their agreement will last for a specified time period and that they will have a chance to propose changes in the employment conditions when their contract expires.

Mediation may or may not be a desirable option for resolving a given dispute. People must assess its strengths and weaknesses and determine whether using it at a given time is constructive.

Rules Affecting Behavior

Some types of disputes are always resolved by applying particular rules. If an employee demands that her supervisor grant her an additional week's vacation, the dispute might be resolved by a straightforward application of the company policy governing vacation leave. If a student complains about her failing grade, the professor can simply point out the rules of this course with respect to grades.

In other contexts, it is not at all clear what rules or principles apply, what these principles require, and the extent to which they are binding. Disputes over affirmative action programs for hiring minority, female, and disabled individuals are plagued with ambiguities about what laws apply and what the principles of social justice require when trying to correct the ravages of discriminatory treatment.

Both the range of available dispute settlement processes and the possible outcomes are restricted by the degree to which issues in dispute are traditionally and systematically resolved by applying clear, agreed-on rules.

Time Constraints for Resolution

Every dispute has a time frame; its sources vary. The nature of the issue may set the time frame. Some issues involved in cases of disruptive student behavior arise quickly and must be addressed rapidly if they are to be addressed at all. Other disputes require participants to spend more time resolving the matter because the issues develop more slowly, involve complex technical analysis, have numerous parties, or concern practices that none of the parties are in a hurry to resolve. Think of how long people have tried to negotiate a resolution of various problems involving Israel and its Arab neighbors.

Other factors can also affect the time frame of a dispute. The participants may create a time frame. If the union declares a strike deadline, then it has imposed a constraint on the ensuing discussions: settle by midnight or it will strike. Laws can set time frames. Business mergers are negotiated in light of the tax implications of specific proposals; if a newly adopted tax law will become effective as of a specified date, then that factor generates a tempo for the discussions. If persons are dealing with politicians whose political power might expire on election day, their talks proceed with an eye on the political clock.

Outcomes

Dispute outcomes differ in kind. They may be written or oral. The parties themselves may implement the outcome, or they might leave the responsibility for doing so to others. The outcome may sever the parties' bond completely or tie them together on a long-term basis. Processes for monitoring compliance may exist either as a component of the outcome or independent of it.

A mediator must learn what existed PRIOR-TO her entry so that she can decide whether or not to commit herself to trying to help resolve the situation. But how does the mediator go about learning what existed PRIOR-TO her arrival? There are some general guidelines that apply to a variety of dispute settings.

Some disputes are reported publicly. Racial tensions and fights among students at a high school are frequently publicized. To begin to get answers to what has happened PRIOR-TO her entry, the mediator can read the newspapers or watch the television accounts of the controversy. In other cases, she can talk with friends, acquaintances, or other sources who know people involved in the dispute or the parties to it.

She can read various historical documents, treatises, laws, or books in order to get the flavor of the dispute. If the dispute involves persons of particular ethnic, religious, or cultural backgrounds, the mediator might read about their traditions and mores. If the issues concern technical scientific matters, she must study them. If the disputants include representatives of a complex business organization, the mediator must become familiar with that corporation's range of activities and its organizational structure.

Some parties are sent to a mediator by an agency such as a court, counseling service, or community-based program following a screening interview. The mediator can review the data recorded by the person who conducted that initial interview to learn about the relationship of the parties, the nature of their dispute, or the results they seek.

A mediator must size up a dispute before she commits herself to serving. Sometimes she can conduct her initial research efforts independently of the disputants themselves, but it is not always possible or appropriate to do so. Sometimes, the only way—not simply the best way—to get answers to what has happened PRIOR-TO her entry is by talking directly with the people involved in the dispute. If the mediator proceeds in that manner, however, she must always remember—and must inform the people to whom she talks—that the goal of such discussions is not to reach a settlement but to explore whether the parties should use mediation or whether the particular mediator should serve.

> *Example 1.* A female employee approaches her supervisor. She claims that one of her male co-workers has created a hostile work environment for her by continually making sexually offensive remarks to or about her. She demands that the offender be fired. The supervisor must acquire information regarding what has happened PRIOR-TO her involvement so that she will be in a position to evaluate the most appropriate way to handle the matter—whether by referring the issue to the human resource department for a formal investigation, by speaking individually with the alleged offender, by advising the employee to file charges with the appropriate government agency, by postponing all action for an identifiable time period, or by meeting confidentially with both employees together in an attempt to mediate an agreement regarding their future conduct.

> *Example 2.* The board of deacons of a neighborhood church informs neighborhood organizations and youths that it will close the church's recreational facilities to use by neighborhood youths because of "continuing vandalism to the property." A group of forty parents and youths protest this decision by entering the church on Saturday afternoon and informing the board members that they will not leave until it reverses its decision. When the board chair refuses to convene a board meeting to

reconsider its decision, the protesters immediately escalate their proposal to a nonnegotiable demand. The protesters contact a local television reporter and tell her of their plight, and her filmed report of the sit-in constitutes the lead story on the 6:00 P.M. local news broadcast. Church parishioners promptly telephone various board members to register their response. Some of them support the board action and others protest it, but all express concern that the matter be resolved quickly so that religious services can proceed the next morning without incident. Various community organizations rally to support the protesters.

At 8:30 P.M. the board chair telephones a woman she has never met who has a reputation as a concerned citizen and effective problem solver. She asks her if she is aware of the situation that has developed at the church; the woman is not. She asks if the woman would help "solve" the situation. The woman responds: "I don't know if I can. Let me talk with you and your board so that I have a better idea of what's happening and what you are prepared to do to resolve it. I'll stop by the church first to inform the people there that I'm going to meet with you and that I will want to have a similar conversation with them afterwards. I don't know if they will be willing to talk with me, but I can't do anything without first meeting with each of you. After talking with both groups, I'll have a much better idea if I can be of any help."

The mediator proceeds to conduct those conversations, learn what has happened PRIOR-TO her involvement, and then decide whether or not to COMMIT herself to serve.

Example 3. A couple decide that they want a divorce. They approach an individual and ask that she serve as a mediator in managing their discussions over financial matters and child-rearing arrangements. In her first discussion with them, the mediator has them talk generally about their situation, their aspirations, and their expectations regarding the mediation process in order to assess whether the parties and the process are suitably matched.

The Decision to COMMIT

The mediator must learn what has happened PRIOR-TO her entry in order to make a very practical decision: Will she COMMIT herself to serving as a mediator?

There are some obvious situations in which a mediator would decline to serve. If a husband and wife asked a mediator to help them resolve their controversy over the methods the husband uses to abuse his spouse or children physically, the mediator would decline to serve. Public policy condemns such behavior; our fundamental individual and political values prohibit letting people decide to beat up others or to get beaten up by others every Thursday night from 7:00 to 8:00 P.M., even if they insist that such arrangements are acceptable to them. Likewise, if members of a terrorist group disagree over which tactics to adopt in seizing a foreign airplane and request a mediator's assistance, most individuals (though, regrettably, not all) would refuse the request.

Other situations are not so clear-cut. The need to decide, however, is inescapable. On what basis does the mediator make that decision? She must integrate the information about what has happened PRIOR-TO entry with an assessment of the following factors:

1. The *commitment* of all parties to the mediation process (C)

2. The *organizational* resources available to the mediator to serve the parties (O)

3. *Mediation's* appropriateness as a dispute settlement process for this situation (M)

4. That *matters* in dispute are ripe for discussion and resolution (M)

5. That *incentives* exist for parties to settle the dispute through joint discussion (I)

6. That the *talents* of the individual mediator are suitable for serving in this particular matter (T)

Her assessment will enable her to make an informed decision as to whether to COMMIT herself to serve. The mediator analyzes each factor by answering its defining questions:

COMMIT:
*Factors Influencing a Mediator's
Decision to Serve*

C:	Commitment of parties to the mediation process exists.
O:	Organizational resources are available to the mediator and to all parties.
M:	Mediation is appropriate as a dispute resolution process for this situation.
M:	Matters in dispute are ripe for discussion and resolution.
I:	Incentives exist for all parties to settle their dispute through joint discussion.
T:	Talents of the individual mediator are suitable for serving in this particular situation.

Commitment (C)

1. Are the parties willing to talk with each other about the issues?

2. Are the parties willing to decide matters jointly rather than simply talking with a view to getting the other side's input before making a unilateral decision?

3. Is each party willing to include all appropriate parties to the discussion?

4. Are parties willing to share appropriate information with others?

5. Are parties willing to use mediation as the primary dispute settlement process for resolving the agreed-on issues or, minimally, to use other procedures openly so that the simultaneous use of different forums will not secretly or suddenly sabotage the mediated discussions?

Organizational Resources (O)

1. Does the mediator have the time to commit to participating in the discussions?

2. Does the mediator have, or have access to, sufficient clerical, administrative, and meeting facility resources?

3. Will the mediator have available from the parties, from independent third parties, or from personal resources adequate financial support to cover the actual costs of the service and, where appropriate, a fee for service?

Mediation's Appropriateness (M)

1. Is the power relationship among the parties balanced enough that one party cannot unilaterally dictate the outcome and force compliance with it?

2. Are the issues being submitted to mediation of sufficient breadth or importance to merit allocating mediation resources to help resolve them?

3. Are the applicable group or institutional rules sufficiently flexible in application or ambiguous in content to permit the parties to develop specific solutions acceptable to them?

4. Do the parties have the resources and talent to participate meaningfully in the mediation process?

5. Are all parties physically and emotionally ready to participate?

6. Are the issues sufficiently tangible so that the parties can resolve them by taking specific, agreed-on actions?

Matters in Dispute (M)

1. Do the respective parties believe that their interests or goals are served by talking with each other?

2. Are the issues in controversy not speculative but developed to the point that the parties can identify them precisely and suggest specific solutions for them?

Incentives to Settle the Dispute (I)

1. Are there incentives for the parties to settle these matters through joint discussions such that personal, institutional, or hidden agenda items will not sabotage efforts to resolve the dispute?

2. Are there incentives for the parties to settle the matters through mediated discussions at this time?

Talents of the Mediator (T)

1. Does the mediator's personality mesh with those of the parties to the dispute so that she will not be a disruptive presence for their interaction?

2. Do the mediator's background, experience, and method of entry (invitation of the parties, with the approval of the governor, assignment by an agency, and so on) secure her initial credibility with the various parties?

3. Does the mediator possess the requisite knowledge base regarding the negotiating process and the various dimensions of the substantive matters in dispute to be a constructive force in structuring the parties' negotiating conduct and developing settlement options?

Once a person has learned what happened PRIOR-TO entry, she can COMMIT herself to serve if she can answer "yes" to each of the foregoing questions. It is then no longer a question of *whether* to mediate, but only a matter of doing it well.

Why Would Disputants Use Mediation?

Parties will never let mediation efforts get off the ground unless they believe that a mediator's presence will be helpful. What advantages do advocates derive by agreeing to use mediation?

Some parties do not trust one another. Although a mediator does not vouch for the credibility of each party, advocates know that no mediator with any pride allows herself or the process to be abused by persons who continuously misrepresent facts, positions, or commitments; no mediator lets herself become a dupe of any of the parties. Thus the parties derive some clue to the credibility of each other's stance simply by virtue of the mediator's COMMITting herself to serve.

Some parties fear that others will agree to negotiate but will then engage in delaying or obstructionist tactics designed to abort the discussions while gaining a unilateral advantage. In mediated negotiations, such fears are minimized. The mediator's task is to establish the tempo of discussions and steer parties toward making tangible commitments to do something. The mediator does not convene the parties simply so that they can meet and confer; her exclusive interest is not to establish a cordial atmosphere or good diplomatic relations, however important those things might be in a particular context. A mediator tries to propel parties into taking concrete action. If they are obstinate or stalling, the mediator terminates discussions.

A mediator can ask important, searching questions without inviting the hostile or defensive response that might erupt if the parties asked such questions of each other directly. A mediator, for instance, wants to make sure that everyone who should be involved in the discussions is present; she will pursue that matter carefully but thoroughly with the identifiable parties. But if no mediator were present and one party told the others that it would not proceed with discussions until all appropriate parties or personnel were present, it would risk alienating them—and escalating their rhetoric and action—by creating the impression that it wanted to divide and conquer its adversaries.

No one likes to be responsible for breaking off discussions, for she may be accused of quitting because she is not getting everything she wants; it also increases the price that party will have to pay to resume discussions. But if a neutral participant, the mediator, indicates that she will not schedule further meetings because she believes there is little prospect for resolution at that time, then all parties avoid blame for the collapse of the talks and can renew discussions later on without first having to assign blame for the previous failure.

The decision to use a mediator has an important symbolic dimension. It represents a tangible expression of one's commitment to resolving issues through discussion. It underscores one's obligation to treat other parties to the dispute with equal respect and concern. It reaffirms one's willingness to take responsibility for making decisions, to be accountable to others for one's actions, and to remain open to considering others' points of view.

The value of such symbolism should not be underrated. Disputes often erupt quickly, parties engage in rhetorical flourishes, and positions immediately become hardened. Finding a face-saving way out of that situation is often difficult. Using mediation is not an acknowledgment of failure; it is not a badge of infamy worn only by those who don't have the foresight to avoid disputes or the skills to resolve them alone. Using mediation reflects a sensitivity to the risks of continued hostility and to the costs of communicating by accident; it represents an informed judgment that mutual discussion with a neutral intervenor might be an effective way to regain control of one's fate.

Of course, parties can pay only lip service to participating in mediated discussions in good faith, while trying to subvert the process in other ways. That simply underscores how important it is for a mediator to make certain a person's actions match her rhetoric. But if a party wants to send a signal to the others that it is willing to explore a resolution acceptable to all, one way of doing so is by calling for, or agreeing to use, mediation.

The overriding benefit that all parties derive from using mediation is that it forces an increased clarity in their communications. A mediator compels the parties to make concrete proposals, identify priorities, and consider trade-offs. She structures the discussions so that parties can explore possible solutions without the intense pressure of having to make quick, nonretractable responses to one another. She helps enlarge the shared base of information on which the parties operate. She serves as a sounding board for a new proposal or idea that one party wants to advance. She alerts parties to occasions where they are overestimating their strength or miscalculating that of their counterparts.

In short, if there is a chance that parties can reach agreement, that chance should be optimized by using a mediator. If there is no chance for resolution, using mediation can at least help the parties know clearly and precisely what constitutes their disagreement.

BADGER

The equation is now complete. Parties have agreed to use mediation; the mediator has learned what has happened PRIOR-TO her entry and has COMMITted herself to serve. Mediated discussions now proceed.

The mediator's method of operation consists of six distinct, consecutive segments: (1) begin the discussions (B), (2) accumulate information (A), (3) develop the agenda and discussion strategies (D), (4) generate movement (G), (5) escape to separate sessions (E), and (6) resolve the dispute (R)—or BADGER.

Put bluntly, the mediator will BADGER the parties into reaching a settlement. The trick is to be able to do this and have all parties still talking with one another at the end.

BADGER:
The Components of
the Mediator's Role

B: Begin the discussion.

A: Accumulate information.

D: Develop the agenda and discussion strategies.

G: Generate movement.

E: Escape to separate sessions.

R: Resolve the dispute.

6
Begin the Discussions

There are two aspects to beginning the discussions. The first involves taking care of the necessary procedural arrangements. The second deals with starting the actual meeting.

Set the Procedural Framework

Where will people meet? How many will be there? When will they meet? How long will the session last? Will there be food? Who will talk first? Who will sit where?

These matters, and others like them, are issues of meeting etiquette. The mediator wants to ensure that meeting arrangements and procedures do not disrupt the substantive discussions. He wants them handled well so that people feel comfortable and there is no awkwardness as they begin to talk with one another.

The mediator begins by taking care of these housekeeping details. Usually he simply announces the rules and makes appropriate arrangements; sometimes, however, these matters become issues of fierce debate among the parties and end up as the first topic for mediated discussion. In any event, no mediator thinks they are trivial. These procedural rules create the framework within which people interact, and one must establish them with care. Like any host, the mediator will receive no compliments for handling them well but will invite interminable haggling and destructive gossip for botching them.

These are the procedural matters that the mediator must handle:

1. Date of the meeting
2. Time and length of the meeting

3. Place of the meeting

4. Number of participants

5. Role of observers or interested groups

6. Room arrangement

7. Rules of protocol (order of speaking, formality of discussions, record keeping, status of outcomes)

Although these seem straightforward enough, they can be devilishly complicated. If a mediator schedules a meeting for 11:30 A.M., does that mean the meeting will last only until lunch at noon? If only one party has to travel seventy miles to attend a meeting in the city where all of the other parties live and work, should the mediator change the meeting site so that everyone must travel thirty-five miles, or should he alternate meeting sites so as not to favor one group? If one group has only two negotiators, but the other has five negotiating team members and thirty "observers and supporters," should the mediator arrange a meeting site that accommodates eight or thirty-eight persons? The mediator must develop these guidelines with a keen sensitivity to the impact the specific rules will have on the parties' interaction and the way in which the rules might tarnish his own image as neutral.

> *Example 1.* Two vice-presidents in a corporation are engaged in a continuing controversy over the type of computer system that will best serve the needs of their respective departments. Their boss schedules a meeting to analyze their concerns and resolve the matter. Because he schedules the meeting for a day that he knows one of them plans to take as a vacation day, one person immediately believes the boss favors him and the other feels at a disadvantage. That perception might generate costly future consequences in low morale and poor productivity, regardless of the outcome of the particular discussion.

> *Example 2.* One party wants to meet immediately, but the other states that he cannot meet for at least three weeks. This tells the mediator how the respective parties view the urgency

of the matter and, perhaps, their perceptions of how much power they wield.

Example 3. A group of fifty concerned citizens are picketing in front of the city library, demanding to talk with the director about his proposed cutbacks in neighborhood branch library services. The director states he will meet with them on the following Monday if they stop their picketing immediately. The citizens tell a news reporter who is covering the event that they have accepted his invitation to meet but have refused to call off their picketing because it is their constitutional right to engage in such activity. A journalist files a news story about the protest and the ambiguity surrounding the scheduled meeting. The library director contacts a mediator, states confidentially that he will go ahead with the meeting as long as the picketing does not result in violence, and asks for assistance in convening the meeting. The mediator talks with the director and the picketers, learns what has happened prior to his involvement, and makes a decision to commit. The first topics he explores with each party relate to establishing the number of persons who will attend the Monday meeting and structuring how the parties will deal with the media.

A mediator must try to make the physical environment in which the discussions occur as conducive to constructive talks as possible. The mediator does not always have control over whether the sessions are held in a comfortable room with decent circulation, heat, or air conditioning; one can easily imagine, though, how much more difficult it becomes for the mediator to resolve a dispute if the parties are shivering in a cold room. Finding an adequate, though not necessarily luxurious, setting helps to put people in a more positive frame of mind. The mediator can almost always make sure the meeting room is clean and orderly before the parties enter.

The mediator *can* and *must* control where various persons are physically situated with respect to one another. He operates according to two principles:

1. Each distinct party to the discussion should have a separate, equal spot in the room.

2. The mediator's position, insofar as possible, should be between the parties, equidistant from them, and closest to the exit door.

The first principle prohibits the mediator from arbitrarily clustering many different parties into only two "opposing" groups. He must not be constrained by the rectangular shape of most tables, which invites him to place parties on each "side." Instead, he must arrange the furniture so that persons with distinct interests are equal, separately identifiable participants in the discussion process. No parent, having just separated four fighting children, would then line them up to talk with each other by automatically putting the boys on one side and the girls on the other. A mediator must not make a comparable error.

This first principle also prevents a mediator from acting according to the erroneous belief that the most effective way to promote peace is to have members of different groups sit next to one another so that they will mingle. Doing this would be a catastrophe. People can have separate, competing interests. They must be able to render moral support to each other or consult among themselves before accepting proposed solutions. The existence of separate identities does not preclude a settlement. If a mediator tries to paper over these differences so that "everyone works together," he undercuts the very dynamic that will help them reconcile their interests. No business executive systematically ignores the fact that various departments within the organization have conflicting or competing interests, nor does he believe that the way to reconcile them is to mix up everyone's work stations so that no one thinks of himself as being a part of a department or section rather than "the organization."

The second principle is important in two ways. First, putting the mediator between the parties and in the middle reinforces their perception that he is neutral. If the mediator is sitting next to party A on one side of the rectangular table and party B is sitting alone across from them, then party B will quickly conclude that the mediator already favors party A. The mediator must place himself equidistant from the parties but close enough to them so that everyone can speak comfortably. Second, by sitting closest to the door, the mediator can unobtrusively pierce a party's frustration or impatience. When parties become annoyed, they may throw up their hands in disgust, shout obscenities, and physicially move toward the door to leave. If the mediator is sitting closest to the door, he can get up quickly and, while moving backward toward the door but still facing all parties, say "I know you're frustrated. I'm not sure we'll resolve these matters here today. But I'd like to give it one final shot. Please, let's sit down. If the matter is not resolved in another fifteen or twenty minutes, then all of us will go home."

Each party can then use the mediator as a scapegoat to return to his chair ("I don't think we'll accomplish a damn thing, but if you want me to stay for twenty minutes, I will") and avoid any accusation that his behavior was boorish or uncalled for. The talks can continue because the mediator had physically placed himself so that he could quickly and without fanfare block the exit.

Assuming that the mediator succeeds in getting everyone into the same room at the same time, he must immediately take charge.

Get Started

The mediator is there to assist all parties to talk about their concerns and work toward an agreement. But he doesn't want them to start to do that too quickly. He must remember that his contribution involves helping the parties discuss those matters in a way that differs from the way they have done so in the past. The mediator won't help them by simply having them replay the same anger and shouting that have been part of their previous, unsuccessful efforts to resolve the issues. He must first help them reorient the way they look at their problems.

The mediator wants to establish an appropriate tone for the discussion. He wants people to feel comfortable so that they can deal constructively with their concerns. He wants to establish appropriate expectations about what can and cannot be done, torpedo the gamesmanship that comes when one party tries to gain an advantage by talking first, and get the parties to have confidence in his ability to assist them. To achieve these objectives, the mediator should start talking—concisely, but without apology.

In formal settings, the mediator introduces himself, disclaims any bias in the matters to be discussed, explains the mediation process, and identifies the ground rules that will govern the discussion. In surroundings where everyone knows one another, the person in charge can modify these opening remarks accordingly. *However the mediator starts, he must make certain the participants understand the goal of the process, everyone's role in it, and how the discussion will proceed.* A teacher does not need to introduce himself to his students, a parent to his children, or a boss to his subordinates; but if a teacher or parent or boss wants to serve as a neutral intervenor, he must promptly clarify everyone's role and the discussion guidelines that apply. Here are some examples of introductory remarks:

Informal. A dispute between two high school students involved in a food fight in a high school cafeteria is stopped by their mathematics teacher, who is on lunchroom duty:

> Jack, Bob—stop that stuff. What's the matter with you guys—did you screw your heads on backwards this morning? Get over here. Listen to me. The two of you are in a lot of trouble for doing that. Unless the two of you work it out right here and now, I'm going to send you to the principal. I don't know what happened, so tell me one at a time. Jack, you start. Bob, don't interrupt; you'll have your chance when Jack's finished. No cursing. No whining. Just listen to each other. Both of you have to be in class in ten minutes—we've got to solve it before then. Jack, begin.

Formal. A dispute between two neighbors is referred to a Neighborhood Justice Center.

> Good morning. My name is Josh Stulberg, and I have been assigned by the Barrington Neighborhood Mediation Center to assist you today. I have not met either of you before, nor do I know anything about the matters that have brought you here.
> Before we proceed, I want to be sure that I have spelled everyone's name accurately and that I am pronouncing it correctly. Could each of you please introduce yourself? Thank you.
> I would like to take a couple of minutes to describe for you what my role will be in our discussion this morning and the guidelines by which I will conduct our conference. The goal of our meeting is to discuss all of those matters that have brought you here and

to develop solutions for them that are acceptable to each of you. I have no authority to tell you what you must do. My job is to help clarify your concerns and examine with you how they might be resolved. If we can identify ways to solve these matters that both of you accept, then I will write the elements of your agreement into the form of a contract, have each of you sign it, and then I will sign it as a witness. Both of you will be given a copy of the agreement. That agreement can be enforced in court.

Let me tell you how we will proceed. I will ask you, Mr. Rodriguez, as the person who first brought this matter to the attention of the center, to speak first; when Mr. Rodriguez is finished speaking, I will give Mr. Tomelli an opportunity to make any comments that he would like to make. While one person is talking, I ask that the other not interrupt him. I have given each of you some paper and a pen; if something is said that you want to respond to, simply jot a note to yourself so that you can talk about it when the other person has finished speaking. This is a private conversation; whatever is said here remains in this room. I will be taking some notes so that I will not overlook or forget any of the matters that you mention; at the end of our discussion, however, I will destroy my notes, so that the only record of our conversation will be the written agreement that we will work to develop.

There may come a time during our discussions when I will want to speak with each of you separately; meeting that way lets me discuss with you in greater detail some of the concerns and possible solutions that we will be talking about. I will let you know if and when I think such a meeting will be helpful. I will stay as long as is necessary to assist you in resolving these matters, and I presume that you share a similar commitment.

Since this room is very small and there are no windows, I ask that no one smoke while we are meeting.

Do any of you have any questions before we begin? If not, Mr. Rodriguez, please tell us about the matters that have brought us here today.

Beginning effectively is extremely important. If the mediator is hesitant, rambling, disorganized, or disrespectful, the parties will not have any confidence that he can help them. If the mediator presents himself as a person who is confident, articulate, and decisive, the parties instinctively will trust him. But beginning effectively is more difficult than it seems. The mediator can omit items, make choices that backfire, or use language that jeopardizes his neutrality.

The mediator does not want to forget to mention specific guidelines because it undercuts his credibility if he is perceived as someone who makes up the rules as he goes along. After all, if the mediator forgot to mention a rule about privacy or interrupting, what else might he have forgotten to mention?

The mediator makes choices when he makes his opening remarks. Does he introduce himself as "Josh Stulberg" or "Dr. Stulberg"? Should he address the parties by their first names, as "Mr.," "Mrs.," or "Ms.," by their titles, or by some combination of these? Should he tell them what authority he does *not* have as well as what he can do? Should he let them smoke cigarettes or drink coffee? Some decisions might immediately alienate one of the parties (for instance, the one who wants to smoke); some decisions can't be changed once they are made (the mediator cannot begin by asking the parties to address him by his first name, Josh, and twenty minutes later demand to be addressed as Mr. Stulberg). The mediator knows that he must make such choices, and he should plan accordingly.

Finally, the mediator must use language that is jargon-free, precise, and consistent with a stance of neutrality. Think of how easy it is to botch this:

JARGON: I'm here as a mediator. My job is to assist you negotiators in overcoming your impasse. (*What is a mediator? A negotiator? An impasse?*)

An experienced mediator of labor–management disputes was invited to serve as an intervenor in a community dispute between the owner of a large apartment complex and a coalition of community organizations that was demanding that some units be reserved for low-income families. The apartment owner described himself as the "housing management." The mediator, trapped in the jargon of his experience, turned to the coalition representatives and asked "the union" for its proposals. The coalition immediately asked for a new mediator.

CUMBERSOME: What I am going to do here today is to explore with you in great detail exactly what it is that brought you here. I want to get your honest feelings about these matters. I want you to speak freely, openly, and forthrightly—don't hold anything back—and tell me in your own words exactly what is on your mind and how you would like to see things resolved. If each of you identify ways to resolve these matters that are compatible with one another, then, of course, the dispute is resolved. But if you identify ways to resolve these matters that conflict with each other—and I would presume that would be the case since otherwise you would have settled this before coming here . . . (*C'mon, man, get to the point!*)

PREJUDICIAL: —Mr. Jones, tell me your side of the story. (*What do you mean, my "side"? I'm going to tell you the truth. Do you think I'm a liar?*)

—Mrs. Austin, why don't we begin by your repeating the allegations that you made against Mr. Castro at the staff meeting. (*Allegations? Nonsense! Those are facts.*)

—Mrs. Lincoln, since you are the person who was harmed and are seeking a remedy, we will begin with you. (*How do you know she was harmed? Is this a kangaroo court?*)

We all say things we later regret. A mediator, however, does not have that luxury if he wants to be effective. He must shape his language to fit his role.

The mediator knows what he must take care of to prepare for and start the discussions. He should plan and practice accordingly.

Once a mediator has concluded his opening remarks, what happens next is spontaneous. The mediator has very little idea what he is about to hear or what options exist. He does not know where the discussion will lead. But that does not mean that he lacks the skills to be of assistance. He will listen carefully and question sharply. He will always use language that reorients the way parties view their challenge. He will consciously deploy multiple options and strategies for directing the discussions.

The mediator is like an orchestra conductor who is directing a group of musicians who are improvising their music rather than playing a composed work. The conductor knows about various forms of music, different harmonic structures, and the sounds and range of the various instruments; his challenge, like that of the mediator, is to get all the players of the violins, trumpets, flutes, drums, and other instruments—the parties to the dispute—to develop their respective parts in such a way that together they create a viable piece of music without leaving various orchestra members scattered all over the floor.

7
Accumulate Information

The parties to a dispute have lived with their conflict. In their various ways, they are familiar with its dynamics and tensions. They feel its pressure. The mediator must become educated about that environment as rapidly as possible.

But the mediator conducts her fact-finding effort with a purpose. She wants to understand how all the parties see their situation. She wants to get an idea what concerns, both substantive and emotional, must be addressed in order for all parties to feel confident that their dispute has been settled. The mediator will not learn everything there is to know about the people she is serving—she doesn't want to. Her interaction with the parties is brief; she will get a glimpse of only a very small slice of their lives. So she focuses on the specifics—on the concrete matters in which they have entangled themselves. She has them describe those details repeatedly and precisely so that everyone knows what they have to work with.

The mediator's job at this point is something like baking a cake in someone else's kitchen: she must know enough about the equipment she is using and the ingredients she is mixing so that when she puts the batter into the oven, the final product will turn out to be edible. The invited chef who complains that the mixer is not state-of-the-art equipment or insists that everyone wait for the cake until she can get her own special ingredients so that the frosting will have a special zing to it is missing the point: her hosts are hungry and they want a cake—a settlement. Not necessarily a *pièce de résistance*, just some cake that they find satisfactory. If the cook reviews what she has to work with and concludes that she does not have the necessary ingredients or equipment to make any type of edible cake, then her hosts will remain hungry. But if the cook is imaginative enough to suggest how she might mix the existing ingredients into a different, though edible dessert, then the hosts may not get a dazzling dessert, but at least they will not starve. The job of fact finding is to discover what ingredients one has to work with and then to assess whether one can make anything palatable with them.

Mediators must do four things in order to fact-find effectively:

1. Listen carefully.
2. Support communication nonverbally.
3. Record notes (in "mediatese") for mediation purposes only.
4. Focus discussion by using different questioning formats.

Listening Skills

What constitutes effective listening skills? There is little in the literature of psychology or communication that illuminates this concept. Most texts simply exhort us to "listen more carefully," meaning that the listener must make every effort to *understand* what the speaker is saying. But there is a difference between *hearing* what someone says, *listening* to what she says, and *understanding* what she says.

If the mediator cannot *hear* what someone is saying, she simply asks her to speak louder, or asks others to reduce their noise, so that she can hear. This is a matter of *audibility*.

A mediator can *listen* to what someone is saying in a variety of ways: attentively, with a look of boredom, while doodling, while listening to music. Listening *effectively* to what someone is saying consists of more than just hearing sounds. One listens in order to *understand* the message the speaker is trying to communicate. To listen effectively is to capture the entire message that someone is sending. Listening skills prevent one from short-circuiting or contaminating that message-sending process. Here are some guidelines that a mediator can follow to make certain that she receives all that is sent:

> *Concentrate*: Minimize distracting activities. Taking notes, drinking coffee, smoking cigarettes must all be done carefully so as not to impair one's capacity to listen.

Monitor the rate: People cannot talk as fast as others can listen. A mediator should not use the overlapping time to daydream about something else.

Be patient: One cannot hear, let alone be certain she has captured what another is saying, if others are not given a chance to complete their statements.

Don't interrupt: One cannot listen while she herself is talking.

Understand first, then evaluate: Often one stops listening because she does not like what is being said or who is saying it. She assumes she knows the argument, and, since she disagrees with it, simply stops listening. A mediator cannot argue mentally with the speaker.

It is important for the mediator to listen effectively, but it is not enough. As when one listens to someone speaking a foreign language, one can hear sounds coming from the speaker's mouth and not be distracted by anything, but if the listener does not know the speaker's language, she cannot understand a thing that is being said. A mediator tries to listen effectively in order to understand what the speaker is trying to say.

There are ways for a mediator to check her understanding of what has been said, although she must always be sensitive to when and where she does it.

She can ask questions in order to clarify previous statements. She can attempt to summarize in her own words what was said. She can, in a separate session with the party, try to confirm her understanding of what the party said by identifying the emotion that the statement exhibits or the priority ranking she attaches to particular items. She might say, for instance: "By virtue of the anger and frustration you showed when discussing issue Y, I would conclude that issue Y, more than issue X, is the crucial matter. Is that correct?"

A mediator should never try to show her understanding of what was said by simply repeating back to the parties in their own words what they just said. For example, at the close of one party's presentation, a mediator should NOT respond as follows:

Let me make sure that I understand what you are saying. You stated that the facilities at the neighborhood school, including the swimming pool, the gymnasium, and art rooms, are adequate and ideal for your children to use after school, on weekends, and during the summer. You said that the families in your neighborhood consist of hard-working, honest, religious people. You said that there are two real reasons why the school district refuses to open up its facilities for use to neighborhood residents during those nonschool hours: first, the school board members are a bunch of snobs who don't understand how difficult it is to have kids engaged in healthy activities because they are rich enough to send their kids to summer camp or enroll them in private lessons; second, the teachers are too lazy and selfish to spend time supervising your children after the class day has ended. You said that the parents in the neighborhood would be willing and capable of supervising the children at their school during the nonschool hours. . . .

Have I understood everything that you have said and proposed? Fine. Now, would the school district representative like to address herself to these proposals?

The mediator makes three serious mistakes if she adopts this style of so-called *reflexive listening* (actually, it is simply parroting). First, a mediator is not simply a tape recorder with a playback button; if she understands what was said, she should show it by summarizing the statements in her own words.

Second, from the moment a person begins to serve as mediator, she should try to reorient the way the parties view their situation. She starts to do this by always describing the dispute in less explosive, nonjudgmental language than the parties have used to characterize their situation. A mediator must not regurgitate the parents' accusation that the school board members are a bunch of rich, insensitive snobs; rather, she should state that the parent group wants their children to have adequate recreational opportunities and facilities during nonschool hours and is proposing that the school district make the facilities at the neighborhood school available to them. The mediator should not repeat the parent group's charges that the school district employs "lazy teachers"; instead, she should note that the parent group proposes to handle the issue of supervising the children at the school by assigning that responsibility to various neighborhood residents.

Summarizing the parents' concerns in this way diffuses any personal attacks and forces the parties to focus their attention on the issues they must resolve—not on other people. In the process, the mediator provides the parties with a new, shared point of departure for considering settlement options. Those who assert pejoratively that a mediator is simply being "diplomatic" when she uses different words to characterize the elements of a dispute fail to appreciate the strategic leverage she obtains through the deft use of language.

Third, parties to a dispute have strong emotions. Despite what the mediator has told them about her neutrality, if one party hears the mediator repeat allegations, assertions of fact, or conclusions in the language of her adversary, then she will conclude, fairly or not, that the mediator believes everything the other has said before she has even given everyone a chance to state what has happened or what should be done. If that occurs, the mediator's potential contribution has been irreversibly demolished. It does no good for her to turn to the party and say: "I'm not agreeing with what she is saying—I'm simply indicating that I understand what she has said." Parties hear such summaries differently, and the mediator is left in the position of "protesting too much."

The mediator might properly conclude that it is important to summarize her understanding of the parties' presentations in order to reassure them that she has grasped what is at stake or to establish her credibility by displaying her mastery over the technical details of their proposal. But she must proceed with care.

The mediator must remember that events affect different people differently. A mediator does not listen effectively if she is always anticipating what someone will say, completing her thoughts for her, assuming that this person's problem is the same as ones she has dealt with before, or "expediting" the process by asking a series of questions. The mediator does not know what has happened. She wants people to state their concerns to her. As they do, they may come to understand each other clearly for the first time. The mediator should keep her mouth shut and let everyone talk—and talk, and talk—until the parties start repeating themselves and the mediator believes she has gained an understanding of both their aspirations and the conditions that keep them from attaining them.

Nonverbal Communication

A mediator can communicate using nonverbal techniques. By turning her chair and body toward a speaker, the mediator reinforces her commitment to give the speaker her undivided attention; however, by burying her head in her notes and gazing out the window while a party is talking, she communicates a lack of interest in what the speaker is saying. Likewise, a mediator's physical appearance communicates a sense of respect or disrespect for the parties and their problems.

A mediator communicates the need for patience by not interrupting others. If she stands up while the parties are sitting and tells them not to interrupt each other again, she signals forcefully to the parties that their verbal exchanges have exceeded acceptable limits. She communicates a sense of urgency by glancing down at her watch before asking a question. If the mediator is the only person in the room who is not laughing at a joke that someone has told, people will wonder whether she is also communicating her inability to empathize with other feelings such as sorrow, pain, or loneliness.

A mediator can also communicate nonverbally her assessment of the credibility of a party's description of events or the plausibility of a proposed solution. If a mediator frowns as she hears one party present her proposed solutions, or if she throws her pencil into the air and pushes back her chair from the table, she is communicating her judgment that the proposal is a disaster. On the other hand, if the mediator suddenly stops writing as one party presents her proposals, slowly and quietly places her pencil on the paper while looking directly and pensively at the party who is speaking, then the mediator is signaling to the speaker and everyone else that what is being said is worthy of everyone's attention.

The lesson is clear: a mediator must be aware of this dimension of her conduct. She must marshal her actions so that she conveys the idea she wishes to communicate. She cannot control how parties interpret all of her nonverbal behavior any more than she can always be certain they have understood everything she has said. At the very least, however, she can make certain that her nonverbal actions are consistent with her verbal statements.

Just as the mediator communicates nonverbally, so do the parties to the dispute. People say things with anger or fear. They communicate a feeling of nervousness or impatience by walking around or speaking with a voice that crackles. They communicate a sense of panic or vulnerability with their eyes, a sense of pride or defiance with their posture. The mediator must be attuned to capturing messages from these communication sources.

Note-taking Skills

It is appropriate for a mediator to take notes. But they are for her purposes only. Any final document reflecting the agreement of the parties will be separate. That fact clarifies the purpose of a mediator's note taking: she records only information that will be useful to her in helping the parties gain a settlement. If the mediator's memory is so keen that she can remember everything that was said, then she has no need to take any notes at all.

What things does a mediator typically record in her notes? She jots down the names of everyone in the room so that she can immediately start addressing people by name. She must be certain that everyone knows what must be resolved, so it is useful to list the specific issues in dispute. The mediator must never be vague or in error about what the parties are proposing for settlement, so at times she may need to record the exact wording of their substantive proposals. A mediator notes the chronological order in which the parties present their respective settlement proposals so that she can detect whether they are displaying flexibility and movement toward agreement or are escalating their demands. It is important for a mediator to note which proposals have been discussed with only one party in a separate session so that she will not breach any confidences and can accurately identify how much more she knows about what the parties are thinking than they know themselves. For all these purposes, note taking is useful.

Taking notes, however, is not the same as making a verbatim transcript of the proceedings. By its very nature, note taking is selective. A mediator does not, and should not, take down everything that is said. We often believe that by taking notes as someone talks, we will listen more attentively, demonstrate to the speaker our keen interest in what she is saying, and affirm the seriousness of the occasion by recording it in tangible form. Rubbish!

When a mediator writes things down, she destroys all eye contact with the speaker, thereby losing her ability to capture what the person is communicating nonverbally. A mediator can become so preoccupied with writing things down that her listening loses pace with the speaker's presentation. Eventually she falls behind and has to interrupt the speaker to ask questions that have already been answered. Since a mediator, at first, does not know where the presentation is leading, she has no idea which matters are relevant to the dispute and which are not. In her desire not to omit anything that might be important, she may record almost everything that is said, thereby converting her notes into the very transcript that she did not want to have.

Most dangerous of all, by taking too many notes, the mediator may become a captive of the parties. Suppose, for example, that during the course of a mediation session involving two neighbors, one states that her neighbor's seventeen-year old son, when his parents are not around, constantly has loud parties where he and his friends smoke marijuana. If the mediator writes that down, what will the parent of the seventeen-year old now believe about the mediator? She will be convinced, with some justification, that the mediator believes that her son has committed a criminal offense. What will the parent do to protect her son's reputation? She will deny the accuracy of the allegations and then charge her neighbor with having engaged in illegal conduct, whether such a charge is true or false; the parent will then wait for the mediator to demonstrate her neutrality by recording *her* accusations as well. This is a prescription for the discussion to disintegrate rapidly into a shouting match.

A mediator wants her note taking to assist, not undercut, her efforts to help the parties reach agreement. She must trust her memory and listen attentively. If she does not remember something that later becomes important, she can always ask the party to restate the point.

Questioning Techniques

Most people, if they talk long enough, say things that are inconsistent with their earlier remarks or suggest areas of possible accommodation. Those are the levers the mediator uses to develop a settlement. Thus the mediator's task is clear: keep the people talking. But the mediator does not want people to talk aimlessly, either; she wants them to focus their remarks. To accomplish that, she must be conscious not only of the specific content of her questions but also of the form in which she puts them. There are five types of question formats that the mediator can use to achieve these twin objectives.

Start-up Questions

How can the mediator get people started talking, particularly if they are nervous or reluctant? She asks them questions that focus on specific events or situations that the party should have no difficulty in answering. Questions including the terms *who*, *when*, and *where* are particularly effective start-up questions:

> Would you begin by describing *who* took part in preparing and writing the report?
>
> Why don't you start by telling me *when* you became a tenant in Mr. Keating's building?
>
> Could you tell me *where* this incident occurred?

The questions force the speaker to start sharing information, but they are not threatening or accusatory in tone. They should help open the door of discussion so that the mediator can quickly follow up with open-ended questions.

Open-Ended Questions

Open-ended questions let the party respond by elaborating on a subject in his own words. Questions that include *what*, as well as phrases such as *tell me*, generate this response.

> Would you please tell me *what* happened next?
>
> Could you *elaborate* on that, please?
>
> Could you please *describe* for me again the events that you said took place last Saturday night?
>
> Will you *tell me* how you conducted the research for this project?

The parties know best what has happened between them, or at least what they believe has happened. The mediator's task is to get them to describe it. Furthermore, the mediator wants to learn quickly what things matter most to the parties. One way people reveal their priorities is through their choice of words and the emotions they use to express themselves. The mediator cannot learn whether someone is angry, upset, committed, or nonchalant if all she does is answer "yes" or "no" to a series of questions.

Open-Ended but Focused Questions

The mediator wants the parties to talk, but she does not want them to talk about just anything. She wants them to focus their comments on things related to the issues in dispute. She may ask someone to answer a question in her own words, but the mediator's question indicates the subject matter the person is to address. For instance, by asking,

> Will you please tell me more *about the party that occurred last night?*

the mediator forces the party to direct her remarks to that incident rather than wandering aimlessly through a protracted history.

Leading Questions

A leading question has two components: first, the answer is contained in the statement of the question; second, the person who is asked the question can respond only by saying "yes" or "no." Here are some examples:

> You were late in submitting this report to me, weren't you?
>
> You left the babies unattended while you were playing tennis, didn't you?
>
> When you leased the apartment to Mrs. Shaw, all the appliances were in working order, weren't they?

A person who asks a leading question accomplishes one of two goals: either she makes the person to whom the question is put defensive, flustered, and uneasy, or she makes sure that she, the questioner, tells the "facts," rather than allowing the person being questioned to do so.

One can readily understand why a lawyer conducting a cross-examination asks only leading qeustions. The questions assert conclusions and are accusatory in tone. They are not designed to foster discussion. They do not generate new ideas. They are designed to establish the anchor points around which all consequences must pivot.

As a rule, a mediator should not pose leading questions. It is a mistake for a mediator (in particular, a supervisor or a parent) to believe she can save time or focus discussion by asking leading questions. Parties to such a verbal onslaught become defensive, terse, and no longer consider the mediator neutral. Such a reaction bankrupts discussions rather than enriches them.

There are, however, a limited number of occasions when a mediator wants to ask some leading questions. But she reserves such questions for her individual meetings with the parties—a caucus. How a mediator uses leading questions to generate movement toward settlement will be analyzed in the chapter on caucusing.

Justification Questions

These are the *why* questions:

Can you tell me *why* that wage proposal is unacceptable to your group?

Could you explain to me *why* you object to Jack's proposed division of project responsibilities?

There are two levels of response to such a question: *substantive* and *perceptual*. Both are important to a mediator.

The substantive response displays the person's rational justification for adopting or rejecting the proposed solution to an issue. "If X is the problem, then Y is one solution because it relates logically to X in the following way. . . . But we prefer solution Z to Y because it advances the welfare of our group significantly more than does solution Y, and the cost of solution Z to you is only slightly more than what you would incur under solution Y." The mediator presses to make certain the party's position is internally consistent and rationally persuasive. A credible response either solves the issues or highlights those concerns that any settlement terms must satisfactorily address.

The perceptual response forces the party to reveal whether the grounds for promoting or resisting a proposed solution relate to the personalities of the parties rather than the logic of the solution. Parties might find a solution plausible but resist it because of who suggested it ("If the finance department proposed it, there must be a catch

to it someplace"); the need to take time to convince others ("I understand that you want to save money by buying computers and word
processing equipment. But that will result in twenty-seven persons
in my unit losing their jobs with no prospect of being employed
elsewhere in the company. I can't go along with this proposal until
I've had some time to talk with my people and prepare them for this
move—the last thing any of us need is for the other fifty persons to
protest this decision by engaging in a work slowdown"); or the fears,
concerns, or dreams that the proposal does not address ("If we agree
to settle this job discrimination complaint rather than contest it
through the administrative hearing and court process, how will we
guard against setting a precedent that gives us the reputation of settling any complaint, however frivolous it might be?") If the mediator
gets this type of response to her question of "Why?" or "Why not?,"
then she must adopt a strategy to meet it, for agreement at the substantive level is a necessary but not sufficient condition for settlement;
parties must be *psychologically* ready to settle as well.

A mediator always acts for a purpose, and this includes asking
questions. She must think not only about what information she is
trying to get but also about how she formulates her question in order
to get it. She does not ask useless questions, nor should she ask a
lot of questions. Particularly in the early stages of gathering the facts,
the mediator must get the parties to present the maximum amount
of information with the least possible interference.

During this early portion of the discussion, the mediator's posture
is to be as supportive and nondisruptive as she can. Her every action
is designed to get the parties themselves to do the talking. The
mediator wants to make sure that she sees the big picture before she
presses ahead. She must have the patience to wait until she is certain
the parties have shared with her the entire landscape of their dispute.
Once they have done so, she moves actively and aggressively to reshape
its terrain.

8

Develop the Agenda and Discussion Strategies

T he parties to a dispute have clashing ideas regarding what has happened or what they should do. Once they have described their disputes, the mediator must manage the discussion in a way that does not simply reinforce their differences. He must take the content of what each party has said, rearrange and reshape it, and then get parties to look at this new phenomenon in a structured way. He does so by first identifying the negotiating issues in nonjudgmental terms, and then designing a discussion strategy to accelerate movement toward an agreement.

Identify the Issues

The mediator takes the information he has accumulated and, from it, distills a series of negotiating issues. Once the parties resolve them, they will have resolved their dispute.

An *issue* is a matter, practice, or action that enhances, frustrates, alters, or in some way adversely affects some person's interests, goals, or needs. Abortion, for example, is a social issue because its practice adversely affects some persons' goals or interests.

Issues are not facts. Whether abortion, for instance, is a widespread practice or is safe only when practiced by persons with a particular training or when performed under particular conditions— these are factual matters that may be important to a discussion and resolution of the issue, but they are not the issue. To take a more trivial matter, how the *issue* of washing the dinner plates is resolved may be affected by the *fact* of who washed last night's plates—but knowing that fact does not automatically resolve the issue.

A *negotiating issue* is an issue that negotiators—that is, identifiable individuals—are capable of resolving with the resources available to them. Employers and unions can negotiate specific wage standards for themselves, but by themselves they cannot resolve the social issue of unemployment. Individual agencies and employees can address issues of employment discrimination by adopting affirmative action programs and policies, but they alone cannot resolve completely the social issue of racism.

A mediator wants to help parties identify *negotiating issues* and then restrict discussion to them. People can negotiate about anything they want: where to eat dinner, what a person's salary should be, what classes to take next semester, where to locate a nuclear power plant. But the negotiating agenda cannot be cluttered with topics that the disputants cannot resolve.

> *Example 1.* A group of students want to protest racism at home and the repressive, racist practice of apartheid in South Africa. They organize a boycott of a neighborhood grocery store in Chicago that allegedly denied an employment opportunity to a black student because of his race. They demand to talk with the store owner about his employment decision and the issue of apartheid. If the students convert their first concern from the social issue of racism into a series of negotiating issues related to that store owner's hiring and personnel practices, then direct or mediated negotiations with the store owner are plausible, for the parties are capable of, and have the resources for, dealing with those matters. Converting the second issue— apartheid—into a series of negotiating proposals is more difficult, for it is not immediately clear what the students or the store owner can effectively do by themselves, given their resource limitations, to resolve the situation.

> *Example 2.* On December 1, three employees of a large corporation in New York City win tickets to attend the Orange Bowl football game, to be held in Florida on the evening of New Year's Day. The personnel handbook states that all employees

are entitled to full pay for eleven designated holidays, one of which is New Year's Day. But the handbook also states that an employee must be present both the day before and the day after the holiday in order to be paid for that holiday. Each employee has used up his allotted vacation time, but it is impossible for them to attend the game and return home in time to attend work on January 2. They approach their supervisor and demand to negotiate the issue of holiday pay; they propose that he change the policy so that employees in his department receive pay for holidays as long as they are at work *either* the day before or the day after the holiday. The demand is misplaced, however, for those individuals do not have the organizational authority to establish policy governing vacation pay.

A mediator must be certain that parties formulate their negotiating proposals in concrete, specific terms. Sometimes parties reach an impasse not because they disagree about the substance of a matter but because one party literally does not know what the other side wants to discuss or how it might act to resolve the issue.

Example 3. A group of parents registered their concern about their children's low reading scores by conducting a sit-in at their neighborhood elementary school. They demanded to meet with the superintendent of schools. At their first meeting with the superintendent's representative, the parent group presented their list of three issues, as follows: "administrators and administrative performance, teachers and teacher performance, students and student performance." District officials genuinely did not understand what they were being asked to consider. The mediators met with the parent group several times over a four-week period; as a result of those meetings, the parent group submitted a three-page, single-spaced typewritten proposal that detailed their concerns. Three months later, the parties reached an agreement.

Finally, a mediator must promptly translate all negotiating proposals into language that is nonjudgmental because negotiating parties, in almost every setting, will formulate their proposals in accusatory, critical terms.

Example 4.

JACK: Dan, I can't work on this project with John when it is *freezing cold* in our offices. There is *no heat* in our building today.

JOHN: C'mon. A little *fresh air* keeps the blood flowing and is good for everyone's health. In fact, if you open the window, it will be *very comfortable* in here.

DAN (the boss/mediator): The two of you must complete your project by the end of the day, so I suggest that we figure out quickly how the two of you will deal with the matter of your *working environment.*

It seems sensible to identify negotiating issues precisely and label them appropriately. The reason it is important for the mediator to do this—and why he makes a significant contribution to resolving disputes in doing so—is that parties often neglect to do it. They are understandably wrapped up in the matter. Frequently, they see only their own concerns and have no patience for listening to the concerns that the others want to address. When they talk, they hurl accusations and blame at each other. The mediator's job is to build a structure within which the parties can channel their remarks. From the information that he accumulates, the mediator sorts out the parties' negotiating issues and uses them to begin to build that structure. Consider the following information that a mediator learned from the parties and examine how he identifies the negotiating issues in nonjudgmental terms:

Example 5. Keith Browning is a high school history teacher. The school year has ended and graduation exercises are scheduled for next week. Ann Jackson, a student in Browning's U.S. history class, submitted her term paper two weeks ago, four days after the announced deadline. Browning gave Jackson an "F" for the paper, citing its tardiness as the conclusive reason for his action. When Jackson spoke to Browning about her paper and the grade, he noted that the paper was very well written, unlike papers she had submitted earlier in the term; he strongly hinted that she had plagiarized someone's work in writing the paper. Since Jackson left that meeting, she has been telling her friends that Browning is a racist; graffiti containing similar charges have appeared on walls in the hallways and restrooms. Jackson is a senior in high school; because she received an "F" on her paper, she will not pass the course, and, since the course is required for graduation, she will not graduate with her class.

Last week, Browning was walking toward his car in the faculty parking lot when he saw Jackson and three of her friends standing by his car. When they saw him, they immediately ran. When Browning reached his car, he noted that the left back tire was slashed and the window on the left side was shattered. The next day, Browning filed a complaint at the neighborhood mediation center, demanding that Jackson pay him $130 so that he could repair the damage to his car that was caused by her acts of vandalism.

Browning is a fifty-five-year-old white male who has taught at the high school for twenty-four years. Jackson is a seventeen-year-old black female. The topic of her paper was "The Biography of Malcolm X." She adamantly claims that she wrote the term paper herself and describes her effort as "the hardest I have ever worked on anything because I was so fascinated by the subject."

Frame the Issues

1. *Reputation of Browning and Jackson in the school environment.* The negotiating issue is not *racism,* for neither Browning nor Jackson can do anything in this situation to resolve that social problem. But the charges of racism and the graffiti have affected Browning's reputation among his peers; they *can* do something about those things and, hence, can negotiate about them. Similarly, the topic of *plagiarism* is not a negotiating issue, but Browning's charge of plagiarism against Jackson affects

her reputation. Since they have some degree of control over how their own behavior has affected or could affect each other's reputation, they can propose things that each might do for the other that would secure their desired status in their school community (of course, proposing solutions and gaining agreement are two separate tasks).

2. *Damage to Browning's car.* The negotiating issue is not *vandalism,* for that term implies that someone deliberately harmed someone else's property without justification. No one, certainly not Jackson, will admit that she damaged the car; and mediated discussions are not a forum in which the primary goal is to make Browning prove beyond a reasonable doubt that Jackson committed the crime of which he accuses her. Browning wants money to repair his car. It is not essential to his getting some money from Jackson that she also admit that she damaged the car; the two elements usually go together, but it is not necessary that they do. If Jackson thought it in her best interest to pay Browning some money for the car even though her friends were the ones who damaged it, she is free to do so. All that is open to negotiation (again with the caveat that talking about it and agreeing to it don't always occur together). But none of those possibilities will arise, in practice, if the mediator simply parrots Browning by directing the parties to discuss the "vandalism" to the teacher's car. In that case, the student will immediately believe that the mediator accepts the teacher's version of the events, not hers, as accurate, and that therefore he is no longer neutral.

3. *Jackson's graduation.* The negotiating issues are not *plagiarism* or *tardiness of paper.* The facts relating to those matters have played a role in Jackson's apparent inability to graduate, but they

need not be decisive. Browning and Jackson are in a position to do things for each other that bear on the matter of Jackson's graduating; Browning, for instance, might consider giving Jackson a passing mark in his course if she passed a test he would devise for her, or Jackson might propose to have Browning give her an oral exam on her paper topic in order to prove that she wrote the paper herself and, assuming she passes the exam, then give her a passing grade for the course. Whether they will or can agree to do any of these things is not yet known, but the topic affects Jackson's interest and, hence, is an issue.

Framing the issues is only the first step the mediator takes. He must now determine which negotiating issue he wants the parties to discuss first. To do that, he must develop a strategic framework for the discussion agenda.

Develop a Discussion Strategy

We can talk about only one thing at a time. If there are two or more negotiating issues to discuss, we must discuss them in some order. Who decides what that order should be? On what basis do we select the negotiating issue to discuss first?

The mediator always establishes the order in which the negotiating issues are discussed. He must be certain that the parties have provided him with sufficient information so that he can identify and frame all the negotiating issues. (Remember that a mediator's notes should be limited to recording and labeling the negotiating issues, not the facts. Such notes will be a valuable aid in completing this next step.) From that foundation, the mediator develops a discussion agenda, governed by one overriding concern: discuss the negotiating issues in the order that is most likely to result in the parties resolving all items on the agenda.

A mediator generates the greatest probability for success by operating on the *principle of momentum*. Simply stated:

Always discuss first the negotiating issue that the mediator believes will be the easiest for the parties to resolve. Proceed thereafter by discussing increasingly difficult negotiating issues, saving the hardest one for last.

A mediator wants to get parties to agree about something, however trivial, so that they begin to develop some forward momentum; with each additional element of agreement, that momentum gains force. A mediator never locks himself into discussing negotiating issue A before negotiating issue B simply because A occurred earlier than B, because A appears before B in the written proposal, or because the parties discussed A before B when they presented their concerns to the mediator. Instead, he reviews all the matters the parties have raised, makes a quick assessment of which one will be the easiest to resolve, and starts there.

Usually, the easiest negotiating issue to resolve is also the least important to the parties. Occasionally, a mediator will get lucky and find that the easiest negotiating issue to resolve is also the most important one to the parties (for instance, two teenagers might agree quickly on which weekend evening each one will use the family car, but disagree about who must chauffeur their parents to the golf course each afternoon so that the car is available for use). Some parties try to resist the mediator's effort to begin with the easier, less important issues; they may comment: "We're wasting our time and fooling no one by talking about those things which have no effect on settling the really tough matters on which we are miles apart." But the mediator must persist; his job is to get a settlement. Collective experience in mediated discussions overwhelmingly confirms the following lesson: piercing a party's resistance to change is done most effectively on an incremental basis.

How does a mediator determine which negotiating issue will be the easiest to resolve? There is no foolproof formula for making that decision, but if a mediator decides incorrectly, he will get very rapid feedback from the parties. But the mediator makes the most intelligent choice possible by matching clues he detects in the parties' behavior to an established set of standards that he uses to organize the discussion agenda.

The parties, for instance, might display a noticeable vigor and intensity while discussing some concerns and exhibit a lack of emotional involvement when mentioning others. They might describe some matters in great detail and spend very little time discussing others.

Or they might use language that indicates varying degrees of commit-ment to a given item ("I want us to *share* our parental responsibilities" is more flexible than "I want us to *share equally* our parental responsi-bilities"). The mediator must be attuned to these nuances and move rapidly to capitalize on them. But the mediator must do more.

The mediator must seize control of the discussion. He does so by applying a series of organizing standards to the parties' behavior and negotiating issues. These standards help him to assess the dispute from different points of view; they enable him to package the content of the dispute in a variety of ways. Each standard is a potential frame of reference for the mediated discussion, and each provides a basis for helping the mediator determine which negotiating issue might be the easiest to resolve. Collectively, these standards constitute the strategies for structuring the discussion agenda. They are what enable the mediator to establish control over the discussion. These organiz-ing standards are: (1) *categories* (C); (2) *nature* of remedies (N); (3) *time* (T); (4) *relationship* of parties to issues (R); (5) *logic* (L). Their acronym, CNTRL (which is the word control without the letter o) highlights their significance. How does the mediator use these elements of CNTRL?

The mediator gets the parties to state their concerns. He identifies the issues and frames them in nonjudgmental terms. He then takes those issues and examines them according to the following considerations:

Categories. The mediator can divide the negotiating issues into vari-ous substantive categories, assess which category of issue or issues will be the easiest to resolve, and then channel the initial discussion to that category. He might divide issues into such categories as eco-nomic/noneconomic; financial/behavioral; financial support/educa-tional expenses/parenting responsibilities; or political/legal/admin-istrative. If necessary, a mediator can develop different categories for different disputes. What he must always consider, however, is whether the issues in dispute can be grouped together in helpful ways.

Nature of Remedies. People resolve negotiating issues by agreeing to do or not to do something about them. A mediator can compare the issues according to what types of things the parties are being asked to do and evaluate those remedial actions according to two standards:

Mutuality of Exchange. Some negotiating issues can be resolved only if all parties do something for one another: offer an apology or take steps to restore personal reputations that have been tarnished by the dispute. This type of issue might be the easiest to resolve, since all parties start on an equal footing.

Degree of Burden of Compliance. Some negotiating issues can be resolved by one party agreeing to do things that are not too burdensome. The solutions to other issues might require one party to do things that more dramatically affect its welfare or challenge its fundamental interests. The successful mediator will start with those issues for which the solutions require the least burdensome acts.

Time. One can assess issues against two dimensions of time:

Chronological or Reverse Chronological Order. The easiest place to start may be with the negotiating issue that developed first in time, or, alternatively, with the most recent issue. The assumption supporting this strategy is that the mediator can rapidly secure agreement from the parties on the first or last link of the chain of issues. The mediator can then use that agreement to put the remaining matters in context.

Time Constraints. Some issues must be resolved by a particular deadline if parties want to avoid potentially more costly or undesired consequences. Other issues don't involve the same time pressure. The easiest issue to resolve normally is the most pressing one, because all parties feel the need to resolve it. If a divorcing couple want to send their child to private school, they must resolve the issue of school tuition payments for that semester even if they have not resolved any other financial arrangements. Failure to resolve it will result in something that both consider undesirable: the child will not attend that particular school.

Relationship of Parties to Issues. Some parties develop an enormous attachment—emotional, political, philosophical, or personal—to particular issues. A union might announce before collective bargaining sessions begin that its top priority for that round is job security; any

CNTRL:
Frames of Reference
for Developing a
Discussion Strategy

Categories:	Separating negotiating issues into substantive groups: economic/ noneconomic, political/legal, etc.
Nature of remedies:	Cataloguing negotiating issues according to how they might be resolved: element of mutual exchange, extent of burden of compliance
Time:	Ordering negotiating issues according to their chronological/reverse chronological development or their urgency to resolve
Relationship of parties to issues:	Dividing negotiating issues according to the intensity of the parties' political, philosophical, or psychological commitment to them
Logic:	Examining negotiating issues according to their status as premises or conclusions of a logical argument

management proposal that might jeopardize that interest will be difficult to resolve. A group of corporate board members might have a very strong emotional attachment to providing financial support to a particular local charity because the corporation's deceased founder felt strongly about that charity's work; proposals to eliminate that contribution in favor of another organization will be hotly contested and not easily resolved. The easiest issues to resolve are those from which the parties are most politically and emotionally detached.

Logic. Some matters are logically related to one another in the sense that agreement on some issues logically requires agreement on others. A parent and child will not agree on the time at which the child must return from attending the high school football game that night if they disagree over the logically prior issue of whether he will be going out at all. A group of landowners might oppose the proposed relocation of the Appalachian Trail because they fear it will split their land and make it impossible to farm; the mediator must clarify whether the landowners object to the presence of an Appalachian Trail in that area at all, or whether they simply oppose the proposed route.

Structuring the discussion of logically related negotiating issues is a tricky matter for the mediator. In some cases it may be more effective to ignore the logically prior issue and begin discussion on its logical consequent. If a child assures his parent that he will be home within half an hour of the end of the high school football game or 10:00 P.M., whichever is earlier, that specific commitment may help him gain agreement on the issue of whether he can go out at all. This approach can lead to success in negotiation even though the issues, logically speaking, are reversed.

The issues can also be related causally to one another. By first examining the basic cause of the dispute, the mediator enables everyone to address the remaining issues more constructively. Although beginning mediators are particularly apt to choose this rationale for shaping the discussion of the issues, it is a dangerous strategy which should be used only sparingly and with great caution. The search for "basic" causes is often a spurious enterprise; further, this approach encourages parties to view problem solving as an exercise in establishing guilt or innocence for previous conduct rather than as a joint effort in shaping their future in light of their past—hence, using this approach results in retarding the settlement-building process rather than accelerating it.

By structuring the discussion in one of these ways, the mediator takes CNTRL of the discussion. He can do so quietly or flamboyantly, but he must do so firmly. Starting the discussion by choosing one dimension of CNTRL does not guarantee immediate success. The parties may make progress on one issue but then falter; the mediator must be flexible, move on, and return later to continue trying to resolve that issue. But the advantage of CNTRL is that the mediator, if no one else, always knows what the next discussion step will be. He establishes a framework for analyzing the dispute that differs from the way the parties viewed it before. It need not be a dramatic difference, just enough of one to give the parties a slight breath of fresh air in addressing their challenge.

The mediator's job is to identify negotiating issues clearly, describe them in nonevaluative lanaguage, and control the order of their discussion. No one will applaud him for doing his job well, but parties will reach an agreement in spite of, not thanks to, the mediator if he does this part of his job poorly. What makes this both difficult and stimulating is that the mediator must make decisions instantaneously. He must gather facts, sort them into negotiating issues using nonjudgmental labels, and measure those negotiating issues against each possible element of CNTRL. Then, as soon as the parties have completed their presentations, the mediator, without pause, must say, "Why don't we talk first about _____"—and, as he fills in the blank, all these tasks must have been completed.

There is one other reason to emphasize the importance of this dimension of the mediator's role. The parties themselves rarely think about these matters. Understandably, they concentrate on getting what they want. But someone—the mediator—must organize and manage the discussion process so that they have an improved chance of succeeding.

The mediator is more than a discussion police officer who simply makes sure people can travel the same road without colliding. The mediator must help create new roads, develop road signs, tune up the parties' discussion engines, and escort the parties on their trip. That is what this "D" component of BADGER—*develop* the agenda and discussion strategies—accomplishes.

But even doing all this does not guarantee that the parties will reach their destination. What does the mediator do when the parties simply disagree about how to resolve the matter that the mediator has so deftly framed and placed in a strategic discussion context? How does a mediator get people to change their minds, modify their proposals, or make concessions so they can move toward agreement?

9
Generate Movement

People often disagree about how to handle particular matters. What is more remarkable is how frequently they are able to solve their disagreements. Something happens that enables persons in conflict to strike a deal and move ahead. But what are those factors that break the logjam? What gets someone to change her mind or agree to do something she had previously resisted doing? The mediator must be conscious of these leverage points and use them deliberately to generate movement toward resolution.

The mediator focuses her persuasive efforts to break up disagreement on four targets: (1) information base, (2) negotiating standards, (3) individuals' behavior, and (4) common interests. If those fail, she appeals to the big picture. Each target area contains a series of leverage points that the mediator can deploy.

Information Base

People change their mind on the basis of the information available to them. A mediator is interested in two things: what people know and what they don't know. She wants to use both dimensions to propel the parties toward agreement. A mediator cannot become too preoccupied with establishing facts, for that can lead to a paralysis of action; but neither can she ignore facts in favor of focusing discussion on those matters that will make people "feel good about themselves." A mediator wants to get people to agree to *do* things; mediated negotiations may be therapeutic, but mediation is not therapy.

The guidelines are as follows:

1. *Facts persuade, so develop them.* If an employer resists granting a wage proposal because she believes it costs too much, then figure out what the real cost will be. Maybe it won't be that expensive, and she will change her mind. If parents are afraid to let a child leave the house at night because they don't know where she will be or with whom, they should find out. They may be less reluctant to let her go if she is participating in a supervised school play than if she plans to hang out on the street corner waiting for some action.

2. *Use the absence of facts to create doubts about what has happened or what can happen.* If a landlord cannot establish with a reasonable degree of certainty that her tenant's child hit a baseball through another tenant's window, then the mediator can use that degree of uncertainty to prod her to reduce her demand from full payment for the broken window to assurances that the child not play baseball in the backyard.

3. *Use inconsistent statements to narrow the problem.* If a person complains that her neighbor disturbs her "twenty-four hours a day" by blasting her record player, but later informs the mediator that she leaves for work every day at 7:30 A.M. and returns home at 6:30 P.M., then the complaining party is not being consistent. The mediator uses that inconsistency not to label the person a liar but to help clarify the problem: it is not a problem of loud music twenty-four hours a day, but one of the volume during those periods when both are home—thirteen hours a day at the most. Subtract another seven hours for the amount of time both people sleep (at the same time, one hopes) and the mediator has narrowed the problem from twenty-four hours to six.

4. *Examine past practices.* Suppose an employee protests her firing for the theft of a forty cent candy bar. The amount in question might seem insignificant. But if the employer's past practice has always been to fire employees for theft of company property, regardless of the amount in question, then the mediator might cite that practice in an effort to persuade the employee to drop her protest.

5. *Challenge assumptions.* People assume many things. They assume other people are rich because of the clothes they wear or the cars they drive. They assume the report was filed late because "Jones

never hands anything in on time." They assume "all grievances can be resolved with an increased paycheck." The mediator must check and challenge all assumptions; an erroneous assumption may be what is blocking an agreement.

Negotiating Standards

A mediator helps people work out solutions they find acceptable. In helping them negotiate a successful outcome, she can try to avoid or forestall impasses by insisting that parties behave according to accepted standards of negotiating behavior. But the mediator must focus on specifics.

1. *Force parties to establish priorities among the negotiating issues.* Parties who assert that every item in a negotiation is of equal significance are either posturing for position or lack a clear idea of their own interests or aspirations. Some things *are* more important than others. People make choices by how they act, if not by what they say. A mediator must look for a party's priorities, even if the party does not explicitly rank them for her.

2. *Compel parties to acknowledge the constraints within which others operate.* No party will agree to do something that constitutes the equivalent of committing suicide, and no negotiating party should expect its counterpart to accept a proposal that has that effect. A mediator must forcefully remind parties that their negotiating proposals must not only reflect their own aspirations but also fall within the resource capacity of their negotiating counterparts.

3. *Develop trade-offs.* Negotiations consist of a series of exchanges. Parties will exchange things only if they believe the items are of comparable worth; that is why establishment of priorities must precede the pursuit of trade-offs. The mediator must prompt the parties to consider their proposed solutions in the context of possible trade-offs.

4. *Pursue compromises.* The one word that gives mediation a bad name is *compromise*. Everyone thinks that a mediator insists that parties compromise in order to reach a settlement. And everyone believes that compromising means "split it in half." Such expressions as "half a loaf is better than none" and "no one is getting everything she wants,

so it must be a fair compromise" betray a critical attitude toward compromise; to compromise carries the stigma of "selling out" one's fundamental convictions.

This attitude is regrettable, for sometimes compromising is the most desirable thing to do. A mediator encourages parties to compromise by forcing them to compare what they are getting in return for their accepting something slightly less than their desired solution to a particular negotiating issue, and to determine whether the exchange is acceptable. There is nothing sinister about that; no one's fundamental interests are necessarily curtailed.

A mediator helps parties get what they need, not what they want. We all dream big, but what we strive for are the things we *need* in order to get along. A mediator helps negotiators succeed by making them focus on necessities, not wish lists. The bigger a person's wish list, the more she will have to give up to reach an agreement with others. But that is no cause for alarm; it simply affirms that the goal of mediated discussions is to get people to agree to do things for one another, not simply exchange either pleasantries or barbs.

5. *Look for integrative solutions.* Sometimes people do not have to give up anything in order to reach a resolution. Suppose there are two furnished, but unoccupied, offices; one is a large office in the interior section of the office suite, the other a small corner office with a view of the town's park. Two co-workers each demand the corner office. The supervisor brings them together to discuss the matter. She learns that one employee wants the corner office so that she can put her plants on the window ledge where they will flourish in the natural light, whereas the other actually prefers a larger office but wants the desk that is now situated in the corner office. They can resolve the question of office assignment without either having to give up anything. Solutions like this are not readily available for every negotiating issue, but they do sometimes exist, and the mediator must encourage parties to look for them.

6. *Prohibit escalating demands.* Once a party proposes a solution to a negotiating issue, the mediator must insist that she not try to improve it later on. Assume that a personnel officer offers a job to an applicant. They discuss and agree on all aspects of the job and nonsalary employment benefits. When the personnel officer asks the applicant about her salary requirements, the candidate states: "I'm

looking for a $40,000 annual salary." The personnel officer replies: "That's fine. We have a deal. I'll confirm our arrangements in writing." Then the candidate says: "On reflection, I really need $45,000 to make it worthwhile for me to make this job move." When a negotiating party escalates her demand in this fashion, it shifts the target for agreement; such constant shifting, or its possibility, makes resolution impossible because one never knows what it will take to strike a deal. A mediator must not let parties negotiate in this fashion because part of the mediator's job is to stabilize expectations. To do so, she must undercut any attempt by a negotiating party to improve its position by increasing its original proposals or resurrecting an earlier proposal that it has since relinquished.

Individual Behavior

Parties to a mediated discussion do not have to agree to anything. A mediator must persuade the parties to accept proposed solutions. She does so not only by convincing them that the proposed solutions are consistent with their self-image and self-interests, but also by deploying a series of maneuvers that psychologically position the parties for agreement. Here are some standard techniques that a mediator uses to generate this desired psychological posture. They are listed in the order in which they meet with increasing resistance; the mediator must remember that her "big sticks" are effective only when used sparingly.

1. *Stroke 'em.* Everyone likes to hear that she is doing a good job. A mediator must reinforce the vanity of all parties by constantly reminding them that they are intelligent, imaginative people who are capable of working out their differences.

2. *Cite examples with which people can identify.* A mediator must teach and persuade by using vivid examples. To be persuasive, examples must be relevant to, or understandable in the context of, a disputant's individual experience. The mediator who must prod an autocratic manager to work more productively with her free-spirited subordinates is more effective if she cites examples of differing managerial styles portrayed in episodes of a popular television series such as M*A*S*H than if she appeals to the published findings of social science research regarding leadership behavior.

3. *Use humor.* Laughing makes people feel comfortable with themselves and their surroundings. It breaks the tension and can help put matters into perspective. A mediator should not use a mediated discussion as an opportunity to polish her comedy routine, but she should not hesitate to inject a humorous remark into the discussions. The only caveat is an obvious one: the mediator cannot ridicule the parties, or any group or class of people, by making them the dupes of the joke.

4. *Try role reversal.* Sometimes a party will change her position or better appreciate a particular demand of the other party if the mediator gets her to analyze the negotiating issue from the other party's viewpoint. A teenager might resist obeying her parents' curfew rules because she believes they are unduly restrictive; but a mediator might get her to reconsider her resistance by making the teenager put herself in her parents' shoes and view curfew rules as safety measures developed by persons whose other daughter—a seven-year-old—was abducted three years before and has been missing ever since.

5. *Exploit peer pressure.* Sometimes a person changes her mind because she does not want to be the only individual in the group who disagrees with the proposed solution. A mediator should capitalize on that need to belong.

6. *Develop time constraints.* People reach decisions when they operate under the pressure of time deadlines. Unions and management negotiate seriously in the face of a strike deadline. Co-workers resolve disagreements over the format of a company publication as the deadline approaches for submitting it to the printer. Some parties resolve lawsuits as they are about to enter the courtroom. The lesson in each case is the same: for all mediated discussions, there is a specified time period within which the parties have the power to resolve the matters by themselves to their satisfaction; once that time period has elapsed, new and unpredictable forces can intervene to affect or determine the result. Parties become less resistant to settlement as they confront the reality of relinquishing control over their fate to those other forces. A mediator uses a time constraint to chasten parties so they will take responsibility for managing their future.

7. *Let silence ring.* Everyone is afraid of silence. A mediator cannot be. People feel awkward when they are in each other's presence but are not talking to one another. A mediator must not rush to fill

the air with chatter. Sometimes one party will relieve the uncomfortable atmosphere by suggesting a possible change in what she is willing to do. The mediator should promptly seize that movement and explore its possibilities with the parties.

8. *Focus on the future, not the past.* When a mediator helps negotiating parties to shape their future, past events involving the parties necessarily influence that design. But the mediator must remember that no one can change what has happened and that the impact of past events becomes less dominant as their details become more ambiguous or disputed. A mediator must not let the parties' competing visions of their past paralyze them so they cannot chart their future.

Suppose a subordinate and her supervisor sharply disagree over whether the supervisor had clearly established the performance objectives which she is now penalizing the subordinate for not having met. A mediator generates flexibility by expanding their discussion from a contest over what happened or who is at fault for the performance level to a consideration of how they will interact in the future. Clearly, that discussion will be tempered by their respective beliefs about what occurred previously; each will propose solutions designed to ensure that similar disputes do not occur. That is fine. A mediator does not want parties to ignore their past; she just wants to be certain they do not become prisoners of it.

9. *Prohibit greed.* In some discussions, one party seems to obtain its favored position on nearly every negotiating issue. At that point, pride creeps in. "I'm on a roll," goes the familiar refrain, and nothing—not even an agreement that gives the party what she needs—will stop it. A mediator must put the brakes on such behavior by reminding that party of how greed contaminates the willingness of others to comply with their commitments.

10. *Exploit vulnerabilities.* Parties to a dispute tend to see things in all-or-nothing terms: "I'm right, you're wrong." One party often insists, self-righteously, that only the others do what is necessary to correct the situation because they caused the problem. But no one is infallible; all parties do things they later regret. These lapses constitute vulnerabilities, which the mediator should attack in order to rebalance the discussion. By highlighting these vulnerabilities, she emphasizes to the parties their joint responsibility for their situation and the need for mutual, not unilateral, action to solve the problem.

Common Interests

If a party to a mediated discussion could get what it wanted without the cooperation of others, then it would have no need to negotiate at all. People talk because they need others to agree, minimally, to refrain from doing anything that will disrupt their activities. Most people cooperate voluntarily only if they are convinced that they are not sacrificing their own interests in doing so. A mediator can persuade parties to do things by pointing out how proposed settlement terms promote mutual goals rather than reinforce one party's gain at another's expense.

1. *Emphasize trust-building dimensions of conduct.* Conflicts erode trust among people, and that loss of trust leads them to demand burdensome settlement terms for fear that any less demanding an arrangement will be exploited. The parent does not want to let her ex-spouse visit their young children because she does not trust his claim that he has cured his alcoholism; the customer wants her money back rather than having the product repaired because she has no faith that the machine will ever work as advertised. The mediator must get parties to do things for each other that help restore a sense of trust. These gestures should not be dramatic; there is no quick fix that will rebuild a person's confidence in another's reliability. But if parties can demonstrate their ability to comply with agreed-on terms, then that conduct serves to restore the credibility of their word, so that a more confident, less regimented relationship can develop thereafter.

2. *Appeal to commonly held principles.* Disputants can usually agree on general principles. It's their application—the specifics—that creates the controversy. A mediator wants to make sure that parties realize they *can* agree to something, and she can best accomplish that by getting parties to agree on general principles. These principles might be simple guidelines: "Can we all agree that we will not interrupt each other or use foul language during our discussions?" or "Can we agree that it is better for us to try to work out this problem among ourselves rather than have someone else [boss, judge, parent] tell us what we must do?" They might reflect fundamental moral concerns: "Can we agree that it is wrong to inflict pain intentionally on innocent persons?"

The goal of these appeals is identical: to get parties to agree to a principle or guideline that has some bearing, however indirect, on resolving the matters in dispute.

3. *Identify joint or shared interests.* When parties to a conflict become preoccupied with getting what they want or piercing the other's obstinacy, they may forget that they also have joint interests. An employer and her employees have a common interest in the success of the business enterprise. Divorcing parents have a shared interest in their children's growth. Residents have a common interest in the quality of life in their neighborhood. A mediator must remind the parties of those elements that bind their fates.

4. *Highlight survival.* Everyone wants to win. But the goal of mediated discussions is not for any one party to win. Rather, it is for all parties to develop a different and shared view of their problem so that they can solve it to their satisfaction. The mediator must emphasize the reality that one party's ability to achieve its objective depends on securing the freely granted cooperation of others; gaining that cooperation requires that each party believe it will be no worse off after accepting the proposed settlement terms than it was before the discussions began. That does not mean that power relationships among the parties do not affect outcomes, or that there is no room in mediated discussions for "tough negotiators." Far from it. But parties must wield their power for some purpose, and the mediator must forcefully remind the disputants that using their power to prevail over the others is not the same as using it to get what they need.

5. *Agree on a process for resolving the dispute.* If parties are unable to resolve any of the substantive negotiating issues through mediated discussions, then the mediator should get them to consider whether they can agree on a different process for resolving their dispute. A feuding couple might agree to seek marraige counseling; a landlord and tenant might agree to resolve their controversy in court. By helping disputants establish what the next step will be, the mediator helps them stabilize their relationship for a foreseeable period of time—a contribution whose value should not be minimized.

The mediator deploys all these levers to generate movement toward agreement. If by themselves or in combination they do not succeed, then the mediator appeals to her final option.

The Big Picture: The Costs of Not Settling

When people become overwhelmed by their attempts to resolve their dispute, they may become impatient, greedy, or self-righteous. This is not dishonorable; it is a common experience for all of us. But it does not help us reach an agreement. It is up to the mediator to remind the parties of a simple fact: obstinacy has a price tag. There are consequences to face if parties do not settle their dispute through mediated discussions. The mediator's job is to force the parties to compare the desirability of those consequences with the proposed solutions they could freely adopt. For this tactic to be effective, the mediator must use it sparingly. She must portray the cost comparison in two dimensions.

1. *Quality-of-life costs*. What happens if the parties don't resolve their problem? People begrudgingly alter their life-styles to deal with the nagging problem. Morale plummets, people brood, and performance deteriorates; annoyance festers and resentment builds. The problem persists; it never evaporates or modulates into something else. These can be the real consequences of living with an unresolved problem. The mediator must ask the parties: Do you prefer this possible state of affairs over that envisioned in the proposed settlement terms? If not, then change your position and develop acceptable solutions; if yes, there will be no mediated agreement.

This appeal is the most powerful tool in the mediator's kit. She must accurately relate the costs of not settling to the realities of the disputants' situation. She must not be misleading or overdramatic, but she should describe the potential situation with an artistry that vividly captures the human cost of continued impasse. Her description must remind the parties of the specific ways they rely on each other's conduct to secure their own satisfaction. After that, she can let the parties make their choice.

2. *Process costs*. If mediated discussions collapse, parties may try to use alternative procedures to resolve their dispute. Minimally, this means that more time will elapse before they resolve their situation. Some procedures may require expending additional resources as well; if a person chooses to resolve a contested employment discharge in court rather than accept the proposed settlement terms offered in

mediated discussions, she will incur additional legal fees and lose time from work (and possibly wages) in order to attend the court sessions. Depending on which alternative people choose, they may be required to abide by someone else's determination of how the dispute should be resolved. These are the tangible costs that parties incur if they prefer continued impasse to accepting the proposed settlement terms. The mediator must describe these to the parties—and then let them decide what they wish to do.

A mediator knows there are multiple tools she can use to try to persuade parties to settle. There is no guarantee that they will work, but they give the mediator a basis for not giving up too quickly. Some issues will be resolved easily and without controversy; others will be more difficult. A mediator's personal experience and knowledge of human behavior will guide her in knowing when to increase the pressure on a particular matter, when to relent and move to a discussion of something else, and when to return for the final push to settlement.

The mediator must not be deterred from employing every appeal possible to badger the parties to settle. She must not feel badly about goading a party into agreeing to settlement terms that the party appears reluctant to adopt; if a party does not want to settle, she has the freedom to decline. The mediator's job is to help the parties reach an agreement, not to win a popularity contest. Her job is to press all parties, persistently and relentlessly. She must make them defend their positions from the onslaught of her attack. And she must remember three cardinal rules about settling disputes:

No one will make a decision if there is any possible way to avoid it.

All specific disputes must end sometime.

No settlement is ever entered into without the parties doubting whether or not they could have done better.

Generating movement is the heart of the mediator's work, the culmination of everything she has done up to this point—beginning the discussion, accumulating information, and developing the discussion agenda—because the goal of those efforts is to establish a context in which persuasion can occur. Trying to do this is intellectually challenging and emotionally exhausting. It is what makes mediating an intensely rewarding experience for the individual mediator.

Mediators use one specific procedure to generate movement that requires separate analysis. This procedure—meeting separately with the parties—combines in microcosm all the discussion strategies and persuasive techniques already analyzed. It is the one mediation procedure that constitutes our conventional image of "shuttle diplomacy." The procedure operates on different psychological and strategic premises from those discussed previously. In many contexts, mediated discussions can proceed with all parties present all the time; the mediator directs discussion, clarifies communication, encourages candor, and tries to move parties toward agreement in everyone's presence. At times, however, a mediator may believe that progress toward agreement will come—that is, persuasion will be effective—only by talking alone with individual parties. On what basis a mediator makes that decision and how she conducts these individual meetings are the matters we must now consider.

10
ESCAPE to Separate Sessions

A mediator chooses to meet separately with the parties—to *caucus* with them—because he believes that doing so will contribute to the settlement process. The purpose in calling for and conducting any caucus can be stated succinctly: *to obtain information and insights that a mediator does not believe he can acquire in joint discussions.* Once such information or insights have been secured, the mediator closes the caucus and returns to a joint meeting.

Caucusing is another tool for a mediator. As with any tool, he must know why, when, and how to use it.

Why and When to Caucus

There are four primary reasons that guide a mediator's decision to recess a joint meeting in order to conduct separate sessions with the parties. Two are psychological in nature, the other two strategic.

Some persons are willing to share information, insights, or aspirations with a neutral intervenor as long as others do not hear what they say. Such behavior is common: a child shares information with one parent about the other parent only on the condition that it remain confidential; students share feelings with deans about a particular professor, but not in that professor's presence; subordinates communicate concerns about their boss to colleagues or resource personnel that they do not reveal to their boss. People's motives for behaving this way are complex, ranging from not wanting to hurt or injure themselves to not wanting to offend the person who is the subject of their remarks. By meeting in a caucus session, a mediator can build on this behavior to shape an agreement.

If people trust the mediator, they share a remarkable range of information with him during these separate sessions. They indicate their priorities among the issues, the range of their flexibility with respect to how particular matters can be resolved, the extent of their resources, their personal aspirations or hidden agenda, the political problems they face with those they represent, or the bitterness they harbor toward the particular persons with whom they are meeting. Sometimes parties will readily strike an agreement without ever sharing—or feeling the need to share—such information with the mediator. At other times, when the parties are making no progress, the mediator must acquire such information to help forge an agreement, and the only way he can do so is by caucusing.

People also have a psychological need for a safety zone—a penumbra of privacy—during discussions. They need time to consider ideas, evaluate what others have said, or brainstorm possible solutions without feeling pressured into making an immediate response. They need a chance to make tentative commitments—"Well, but if I did that, would he be willing to do this?"—without fear that others will immediately interpret such remarks as definitive concessions. By meeting in a caucus session, a mediator creates this safety zone for each participant.

Strategically, a mediator must chip away at a party's rigidity. Sometimes the only way he can generate flexibility is by firing a series of pointed, stinging questions at the party. But the danger in a mediator's doing that in everyone's presence is twofold: first, he will generate a defensive response that will reinforce the parties' differences; second, he will undercut the parties' perception of his own neutrality. By asking such questions in a caucus format, the mediator can avoid these pitfalls.

Example 1. A dissatisfied customer states that his $300 suit was irreparably damaged while being handled by employees at the dry cleaner; he demands full reimbursement. The store owner claims that the damage consisted only of a slight tear in the jacket sleeve, which his tailor had repaired; as a "sign of good will," however, he offers to settle the matter by giving the customer $10 worth of credit toward future dry cleaning charges. Both parties hold firm. At some point the mediator must ask the customer directly whether he is willing to accept less money than he is demanding in order to reach a settlement. But if the parties have been adamant in their positions up to that point, then the mediator knows what the answer to his question will be—a resounding "no". So he must not ask it in everyone's presence. If the mediator asks the customer that question in a caucus, however, in conjunction with a penetrating review of the costs of not settling, he might provoke a different response.

Similarly, the mediator probes sharply for weaknesses or loopholes in a party's position in order to convert them into bases for developing settlement terms. But he cannot engage in such an attack on a party's proposal without making that party feel that the mediator has turned against him and is no longer neutral. Conversely, if the other parties witness the mediator engaged in such an attack, they may believe he has now become their advocate, and may begin to take comfort in the belief that they do not need to modify their own position in order to reach a settlement. The mediator escapes both horns of that dilemma by pursuing his analysis in separate meetings.

So a mediator has sound bases for meeting separately with the parties. He need not feel locked into conducting all discussions in everyone's presence. But he must recognize that meeting separately creates special obligations and challenges.

Both the timing of a caucus session and the choice of whom to meet with first are dictated by the purpose the mediator wants to promote. These general purposes are captured by the acronym ESCAPE: (1) *explore* settlement options (E); (2) *signal* warning signs (S); (3) *confirm* movement (C); (4) *attack* recalcitrant party (A); (5) *pause* (P); and (6) *evaluate* (E).

Explore Settlement Options. After some period of time, parties engaged in joint discussion begin to repeat themselves; they reject all proposed solutions. The mediator must gain a better understanding of why particular options are unacceptable or provide an atmosphere in which parties can explore a variety of possible solutions without having to make an immediate decision to adopt one. He calls for a caucus. From a substantive viewpoint, it does not matter which party

---

ESCAPE:
Meeting Separately with the Parties

E: Explore settlement options.

S: Signal warning signs.

C: Confirm movement.

A: Attack recalcitrant party.

P: Pause.

E: Evaluate.

---

the mediator meets with first. The mediator's choice is frequently guided by such considerations as which party is seeking to alter the status quo or which party believes itself to be at an emotional, political, or power disadvantage; meeting first with those persons is frequently interpreted by them as bestowing on them a sense of legitimacy and equality with all other participants—which puts them at ease and encourages them to be flexible.

Signal Warning Signs. Parties miscalculate how their conduct affects others. They misread or are oblivious to people's reactions to their gestures, language, and behavior. The mediator must quickly correct that situation.

Example 2. In the middle of a budget negotiation, one party accused the other of "killing innocent children by denying youth programs a larger share of the available monies." The mediator called for a caucus and met first with the budget director. The first words of the caucus exploded out of the budget director's mouth: "If that s.o.b. accuses me again of being a child killer, I'll throw him out on his behind and stop all discussions." Before returning to the joint session, the mediator spoke with the accusing party and forcefully instructed him to cease making such charges.

A mediator, of course, does not have to wait to be told that certain conduct is deeply offensive. If he knows that one party's conduct will alienate the others, then he can declare a caucus and meet first with the offending party to convey that message firmly.

Confirm Movement. Parties signal a change of position in many ways. Some are explicit: "We have a new wage proposal for you: we are now offering a 5 percent wage increase for each year of the contract." Other shifts are subtle: the proposal that "Every community group that uses the school facilities must assume *primary responsibility* for cleaning up" becomes "Every community group that uses the school facilities must assume *responsibility* for cleaning up when it is finished." Sometimes a party signals movement simply by no longer talking about an issue it had raised earlier in the discussion. A mediator who wants to be certain the movement is real rather than an oversight can declare a caucus and meet first with the party that appears to have made the change.

Attack Recalcitrant Party. At some point in the discussions, a mediator knows which party must change its position on a specific issue in order for a settlement to come about. Suppose the owner of the dry cleaning store, in the example cited earlier, informs the mediator after a lengthy discussion that he will pay no more than $75 to his dissatisfied customer; to pay any more, in his judgment, would make the cost of settlement exceed any costs he might incur for not settling. The customer, meanwhile, has "dropped his demand" to $250. If the mediator senses that the store owner is very firm in his position, then he must use every persuasive strategy that is necessary to convince the customer to accept something less than $250. The mediator attempts to change the customer's position not because he believes the customer is wrong in maintaining it or thinks the store owner's offer is a fair settlement; he does so because he is convinced there will be no agreement unless movement comes from the customer. The mediator declares a caucus and meets first with the defiant customer; by forcefully portraying to the customer the costs of his continued recalcitrance, the mediator tries, as one police officer deftly put it, to drill that party a set of brains.

Pause. Parties need time to consider comments and proposals or to reconsider their own position. They do not need a mediator with them; they need to escape to their safety zone. The mediator declares such a caucus after one party has made a new proposal or as the parties are approaching stalemate. He indicates to them the specific topics that he wants each of them to consider in their separate meetings and then directs them to a place where they can be alone. The meeting is structured substantively and has a time limit, but it is conducted without the mediator.

Evaluate. A mediator needs time to evaluate whether progress is being made or to design a plan of action. Although he should keep such recesses to a minimum, he must not hesitate to call for one if the need arises. When announcing such a session, he indicates to the parties that he is declaring a recess in order to review his notes and evaluate how best to proceed; he invites them to do the same. The mediator ushers the parties to a place where each can be alone; he then returns to the conference room to determine what his next steps should be.

A mediator who calls for a caucus but cannot identify its general purpose is abusing this valuable tool. A mediator should ESCAPE from the joint discussion only if caucusing constitutes the most likely avenue for helping the parties reach a consensus.

How to Conduct a Caucus

Four principles shape the way a mediator conducts the caucus:

1. All discussions are confidential unless the party authorizes the mediator to share their content.

2. The goal of every caucus is to discuss matters that are relevant to developing a settlement.

3. The mediator meets with every party each time he calls for a caucus.

4. The amount of time a mediator spends with each party in a caucus need not be identical.

Within this framework, a mediator proceeds as follows. The mediator indicates to all parties that he wants to meet with them separately. He states the order in which he will talk with them, indicates the approximate length of time he will spend with each party, and excuses everyone but the party with whom he will meet.

The Initial Caucus Session

The mediator immediately does two things: first, he notes the starting time of that caucus session; second, he organizes his notes so that he separates the information he acquires during a separate session from that obtained during the joint meetings. The reasons for doing these are obvious: time goes very rapidly when conducting a caucus, so what seems like fifteen minutes to a mediator may actually be forty-five minutes. The mediator must remember that time passes slowly for those parties who are waiting and he must be vigilant in keeping them engaged. Since the mediator gains leverage by capitalizing on the knowledge gap that exists among the parties, organizing his notes in the manner suggested here helps him to pinpoint which party knows what at any given point in time.

The mediator starts every caucus by stating that the discussion is confidential; he will not share any information with the others unless the party authorizes him to do so. But the mediator also emphasizes that the purpose of the discussion is to explore ways to resolve the matters; it is not simply a session for divulging racy gossip.

By the time the mediator completes that statement, he must not only know what he wants to learn in this particular caucus but also have developed a plan of attack for getting it. And the mediator's plan of attack combines strategies for developing a discussion agenda with persuasive strategies for generating movement. Consider the following scenario:

> *Example 3.* XYZ Corporation manufactures jet engine components for military aircraft. Smith and King, skilled mechanics who work next to each other at XYZ's plant, approach their supervisor. Smith accuses King of intentionally damaging the tools in his personal toolkit; he demands $450 as reimbursement. King accuses Smith of creating a hostile work environment by incessantly making racial slurs; in addition, he charges Smith with recklessly endangering his safety

by intentionally distracting King just as he is drilling grooves that require extraordinary precision. Both agree that they should not continue to work next to each other, and each demands that the other be reassigned to work the second shift.

King has worked at XYZ Corporation for six years, the last two as a mechanic; Smith has worked his entire five-year tenure at XYZ Corporation as a mechanic. The supervisor decides to meet separately with each employee; he talks with Smith first. His purpose is to learn whether there are any circumstances under which Smith is willing to work the second shift. What should he talk about with Smith, and which issues should he discuss first?

Depending on the personalities of Smith and King as well as the general tenor of the discussion, the supervisor could develop his plan of attack around any of the following starting points:

1. *Smith's issue—damaged tools:* This is the matter that seems to concern Smith the most. The supervisor's strategy in starting here is to put Smith at ease by demonstrating a concern about meeting his interest with regard to his personal tools. Even if there is no immediate resolution of that matter, Smith will at least feel comfortable in knowing that the supervisor understands what he wants. Then the supervisor can press hard in trying to generate flexibility on the matter of the shift assignments; he has improved his chance for success because the previous discussion has left dangling the possibility of a trade-off on reimbursement for the tools in exchange for agreement to a change in work shifts.

2. *Areas of vulnerability—seniority:* If Smith is a particularly arrogant individual who is trying to blame King for their predicament, then the supervisor might want to equalize the parties by immediately discussing those issues whose resolution could block Smith from having any of his interests met. Following this strategy, the supervisor would begin by discussing the issue of shift assignments and would point out to Smith that company policy favors making shift assignments, all other things being equal, on the basis of companywide seniority, not department-based seniority. Fearing that he might be

assigned to that second shift, Smith might indicate a willingness to work that shift if King reimburses him for the damaged tools.

3. *Areas of mutual interest—safety measures:* Both men agree that they should not continue to work next to each other. Having established that someone will move, but deferring discussion about who will move, and when, the supervisor can have Smith identify what he and King can do in the immediate future to prevent property damage and ensure their physical safety. The supervisor might then discuss the matter of the damaged tools. With Smith obtaining some sense of security in these two areas, the supervisor can then probe the matter of changing one person's shift assignment by discussing first its timing (next week? after this specific project is completed in one month?) and then whose shift will change.

4. *General principles—value of positive work environment:* The supervisor could begin by discussing basic principles that are probably noncontroversial: the need to treat each other with respect and not endanger each other's personal safety or property. With those commitments as the frame of reference, the supervisor could then pursue one of the aforementioned strategies.

5. *Costs of not settling—loss of job:* The supervisor might try to create an atmosphere of urgency by immediately reminding Smith of what will happen if there is no agreement on who will work the second shift: no reimbursement for the damaged tools, possible disciplinary actions against both Smith and King, and a unilateral decision by the supervisor as to which shift each person will work. Against this background, the supervisor might then focus on the issue of shift assignments and ask Smith to state those conditions under which he might be willing to move to the second shift.

There are other options a mediator could deploy. A mediator should conduct a caucus in the same purposeful way that he directs other aspects of the discussion. A caucus is not a "rap session." The mediator does not "wing it" in a caucus. He calls for a caucus to gain information or insights that will contribute to developing a settlement. By integrating a selected strategy for generating movement with a developed discussion agenda, he gets the data he wants.

The mediator closes each caucus by asking the party to identify anything they have discussed that he does not want the mediator to share with the other parties. (Notice the mediator's translation of his original opening remarks regarding confidentiality: the assumption is that the mediator can use anything that is not flagged to develop a settlement.) With the answer in hand, the mediator moves to the next meeting.

The Second Caucus Session

The mediator will always meet in caucus with each of the parties to a dispute before reconvening them in a joint session. He does this to maintain his image as neutral and impartial. Separate meetings arouse suspicion that private deals are being made, and a mediator who conducts a substantial majority of such sessions with only one party inflames that fear. However, the length of time the mediator spends with all parties need not be identical; the nature and length of these subsequent caucuses is determined by the purpose for which the mediator originally called for the caucus. If, for instance, the mediator declared a caucus in order to confirm movement by one party or to challenge a recalcitrant party to modify its posture, then once he has finished his initial caucus session, his mission is accomplished; there is no substantive need for him to meet with any of the other parties in separate session. But to preserve his image as impartial, the mediator must extend to each of the other parties the courtesy of meeting alone with each of them. He approaches each of them separately and asks whether there is anything the party would like to discuss with him before he brings everyone together. If the party raises some concerns, the mediator listens and responds accordingly; if the party has nothing new to mention, as is normally the case, the mediator invites everyone back into joint session.

However, if the mediator declared the original caucus in order to explore possible settlement options, then he will find himself conducting a series of consecutive caucus sessions with the various parties. When that happens, his challenge is to conduct the sequential sessions in a way that enables him to communicate information, honor confidences, and explore the acceptability of specific settlement terms without disclosing known offers of movement. How does he do that?

Protecting Offers of Movement. A mediator does not conduct caucuses simply to tell one party what the others have said to him privately. The mediator develops his strategy and discussion agenda for subsequent caucuses in the same manner that he follows when conducting the first caucus session. Now, however, he must incorporate into his plan an indirect test for determining whether the terms of agreement that one party has now tentatively accepted are satisfactory to the other.

Using the last example discussed previously, suppose Smith told the supervisor in his initial caucus that he would work a different shift immediately if King would pay some amount toward the repair of the damaged tools. The supervisor's job is to find out if that proposed arrangement is acceptable to King. How should he proceed?

Suppose the supervisor conducts his caucus with King by selecting the fifth strategy listed; that is, he begins by reminding King of the cost of not settling. Against that backdrop, he moves to a discussion of the damaged tools and suggests emphatically that there will be no agreement—the costs of not settling will obtain—unless King is willing to do something to help Smith replace his damaged tools. King, if he was assured that the discussion was confidential, might reveal many things to the supervisor: that he damaged the tools because he was fed up with Smith's racist barbs, that he himself did not damage the tools but that he had prompted his friends to do so, or that he did not damage the tools intentionally but had been drinking beer at lunch (in violation of company rules) and smashed them in a drunken stupor. King might conclude by stating that he is willing to pay Smith some money for the repair or replacement of the damaged tools but only on two conditions: that he does not have to admit to Smith that he damaged them, and that Smith works the second shift.

Eureka! An agreement is at hand. The supervisor now knows that Smith and King will resolve their dispute as long as the amount of money King is willing to pay is acceptable to Smith.

Of course, this strategy might not have generated such a welcome response. Or the supervisor might have approached the discussion from a different angle.

But the supervisor would invite disaster if he were to begin his caucus with King as follows:

SUPERVISOR: Smith is willing to work the second shift if you pay him something for the damaged tools. Is that acceptable?

Why is this approach a disaster? If the supervisor says this, King immediately knows that Smith will do what King wants him to do—work the second shift; King will now try to get Smith to do that without giving him anything substantial in return. Thanks to the supervisor's bungling, King will have acquired a powerful incentive for digging in his heels and testing whether he can force Smith to capitulate.

If, however, a mediator conducts each caucus not by explicitly testing the acceptability of the other's proposals but, rather, by structuring the discussion to learn what specific arrangements each party needs in order to settle, then he will discover whether there is a gap or an overlap in their proposed settlement terms without inadvertently aggravating their tensions.

Protecting the Source. Testing the acceptability of settlement terms in an indirect manner does not mean that a mediator should be coy. Sometimes he needs to find out clearly whether one party will accept specific terms that the mediator knows are acceptable to the others. How can he do this without giving away the store? There are two options: he can propose the settlement terms in a hypothetical format, or he can adopt the proposal as his own. Here is how these approaches would work when the supervisor caucuses with King:

SUPERVISOR (Option 1): Let's consider the following possibility. What if Smith were to work the second shift and you were to pay him some amount of money toward the repair or replacement of the damaged tools. Would that be an arrangement you could live with?

SUPERVISOR (Option 2): I don't know if this arrangement would be acceptable to either of you, but let me toss out the following idea for each of you to consider. Suppose he were to work the second shift and you were to pay him some amount of money toward the repair or replacement of the damaged tools. Could you live with that arrangement?"

What are the likely responses to such questions? If King finds this an acceptable format, he can respond accordingly. If he tried to accept only part of it ("I'll agree that Smith should work the second shift, but I won't pay him any money for the damaged tools"), then the supervisor can either remind King that the idea involved two dimensions or force King to provide his reasons for such objections (the justificatory questions) so that he has a better understanding of what it will take to get an agreement. If King thinks the entire idea is stupid, he can simply blame the supervisor for it rather than becoming furious at Smith for making "one more selfish attempt to squeeze me for the money."

Of course, King might respond to the proposed questions by asking sharply: "Did Smith tell you he would agree to this?" The supervisor must respond: "I'll have to talk to him about it again, but I won't even do that if it is not acceptable to you." Or the supervisor, wanting to communicate a sense of optimism, might hedge his response: "I think I can get him to accept it if you give me something meaningful to work with in terms of compensation for the damaged tools." The supervisor does not lie to King by denying that he has discussed this possibility with Smith, nor does he become defensive and tell King it is none of his business. But he must respond in a way that enables each party to evaluate the proposed settlement terms without knowing whether the terms are acceptable to the other.

By protecting the source of the settlement proposals in either of these two ways, a mediator allows for one other possibility: he preserves for the parties the option of rejecting those terms now but accepting them later in the discussion. A mediator must remember that parties have only one chance to accept or reject a formally communicated proposal; once the proposal is rejected, it cannot be revived. Therefore, a mediator must shape his conduct and language in the caucus to be consistent with an informal, but directed, exploration of settlement options.

> *Example 4.* A tenant informs a mediator during a caucus that he is willing to pay $100 to satisfy all claims for back rent. The mediator, in a caucus with the landlord, floats that possibility as a hypothetical proposal; the landlord rejects it. Two hours later the landlord might have a different appreciation of the tenant's problems or a realistic view of what he might be able to get; suddenly, a $100 settlement may be more attractive and can be revived as a possible settlement option.

If, however, the mediator had erred by originally telling the landlord that "the tenant said he would pay you $100 to settle," and the landlord had rejected the proposal, then any subsequent settlement figure would have had to be greater than that formal proposal of $100; that increase, however, small it may be, might constitute the difference between a settlement and a stalemate.

Displaying the Agreement

By conducting a caucus, the mediator becomes the first person to know when the parties have reached a settlement. His task is not over. He must decide how to reveal those terms of agreement to the parties. He has two options: he can have the parties propose them to each other, or he can reveal them and simply ask the parties to confirm their acceptance of them.

By the Parties. There is a decided advantage in having the parties communicate directly to each other what they are willing to do to resolve the dispute. They are the ones who must live with the solution. They must be able to get along with each other at least to the degree called for under their settlement terms. They must feel that the agreement is one they find acceptable rather than one that is being thrust upon them. They begin to rebuild or restore their confidence in the other party's commitment to comply with the agreement by hearing the other state explicitly what he is pledging himself to do to resolve the dispute.

If the mediator adopts this approach, he reconvenes the parties following the caucuses and directs them to indicate to each other what they are prepared to do to resolve the remaining issues in dispute. In the foregoing example, the supervisor would reconvene Smith and King and speak as follows:

SUPERVISOR: I'd like to have each of you tell the other what you discussed with me in our separate discussions regarding how the matters of the damaged tools and shift assignments can be resolved to your satisfaction. Smith, why don't you speak first?

The potential disadvantages to proceeding in this way are obvious: the party who speaks might propose terms that differ from those he had accepted during his caucus, or he might preface his statement with such derogatory or self-serving remarks that the other party ends up rejecting terms he had previously indicated were acceptable. It does not matter if the speaker does this deliberately or inadvertently. Either way, the agreement is jeopardized. How can the mediator sidestep that pitfall?

By the Mediator. Sometimes the mediator must tie down the agreement securely and then move on; this is particularly true in situations where the mediator senses that the parties are agreeing to do what is necessary to resolve the dispute but remain bitter toward one another or resent some of the settlement terms. To accomplish this, the mediator reconvenes the parties, identifies the unresolved issues, indicates what each party is willing to do or accept to resolve that issue, and asks the parties to confirm his statement. What this approach lacks in fostering communication, it compensates for by being precise and succinct:

SUPERVISOR: With regard to the matter of the shift assignment, Smith agrees to work the second shift beginning next week and King will remain on the first shift. Is that right?

Whether we are trying to prevent acts of violence at a protest march, resolve complaints of sexual harassment at the workplace, reduce the possibility of the outbreak of gang wars, assist neighborhood residents in working out differences with government agencies over planned commercial development, or help our children solve problems between them, we often choose to talk with each party alone and then with everyone together. Caucusing can be very useful. It generates a sense of confidence and intimacy between the party and the mediator. It invites candor and encourages an uninhibited exploration of solutions.

But caucusing has drawbacks as well. It consumes enormous amounts of time. It transfers the responsibility for communication from the parties to the mediator. It blocks the development of creative energy that develops from a lively exchange and interaction among discussants.

So a mediator must use caucusing deliberately and selectively. He must not hesitate to use it when appropriate, but he must realize that he does not need to use it to resolve every dispute. Caucusing is a tool. Just because a person has a hammer, that does not mean he should treat everything else in the world as the head of a nail.

11
Resolve the Dispute

A ll mediated discussions must eventually end. One hopes that parties will conclude their discussion believing that the agreed-on settlement terms promote or secure their respective interests and concerns. But sometimes there is no mutually acceptable resolution of the negotiating issues.

Whatever the outcome, the mediator plays an active role in staging the final act.

Outcome A:
No Resolution on Substantive
or Procedural Issues

Some mediated discussions end without any resolution of the negotiating issues. No mediator should try to camouflage that fact. But she must try to make certain the parties leave the discussions without feeling any more bitterness toward one another than they did before the meeting and with a clear idea of their options.

The mediator does not want the parties to leave feeling incapable of dealing with their situation in the future. She can discharge her duty as scapegoat at this juncture by expressing to all parties her regret that she was unable to help them resolve their dispute. Even if the mediator believes that the parties are ignorant, stubborn fools, she does not tell them so, but attributes their lack of success to her own inability to help them. This does not fool anyone, but it does allow the parties to leave the discussion without undue anger or despair.

The mediator also highlights what the parties have accomplished during their talks. The absence of a settlement does not mean the discussions were useless. The mediated discussion may well have clarified issues more precisely, developed a more credible information base as a basis for future decisions, canvassed the strengths and weaknesses of various settlement options, and improved communication among the parties by piercing inflammatory rhetoric. These are not insignificant elements of progress; although the mediator must not exaggerate their value, she should bring them to the parties' attention so that they do not leave the meeting wallowing in frustration.

The mediator should always commend the parties for their efforts to resolve the issue, express her hope that they will find a way to resolve it to their satisfaction, and end the meeting on a courteous note.

Outcome B:
Agreement on Procedural Issues Only

When mediated discussions collapse, the most destabilizing factor is that one party can now act unilaterally and without notice. Such actions invariably alter the status quo and force the other party to escalate its conduct in order to protect its interest. This scenario is amply demonstrated in the regrettable situation wherein parties to a divorce proceeding fail to agree on separation terms and, before a judicial decree is rendered, one spouse secretly takes the children out of the jurisdiction.

Even if the mediator does not succeed in helping the parties reach agreement on the substantive issues in dispute, she tries to have them agree on a process for resolving them. The mediator may be able to get them to agree to resolve the matters in court, to obtain counseling, to seek legislative reform, or to establish a truce. The value of such an agreement is that it establishes reliable expectations on which to base short-term plans.

Outcome C:
Agreement on All or Some Substantive Issues

The primary goal of mediated discussions is to have disputing parties resolve substantive issues in a mutually acceptable way. If that is achieved for all the issues in dispute, then the parties congratulate themselves and move ahead.

If the mediator helps the parties resolve some but not all of the substantive issues, then she has the parties explore two options: (1) agreeing on a process for handling the unresolved substantive issues, or (2) agreeing to implement those matters on which they have agreed even though other substantive issues remain unsettled. If the mediator can get the parties to agree on a process for handling the unresolved substantive issues (for example, sending the matter to a committee for study), then the parties, in fact, will have resolved all outstanding matters; they will have a complete agreement. But what if that move does not succeed?

In some contexts, such as when a union and management are negotiating terms of a new collective bargaining agreement, the parties adopt a procedural framework that makes final agreement on any one issue contingent on resolution of all matters; everything is "tentatively agreed to" until all elements of the package are adopted. If, for example, parties agree on an expanded vacation schedule, increased health benefits, and less cumbersome work rules, but cannot agree on new wage rates, then they have no agreement on any issue. Obviously, a mediator tries to persuade the parties to reach agreement on wages so they do not lose the benefits they have provisionally secured. She does this by pointing out to them the costs of not settling. Under this procedural framework, however, if an agreement on wages is not reached, then all bets are off.

Unless the parties have agreed in advance to such an all-or-nothing governing procedure, then whether parties implement those substantive matters that they have resolved, even though other issues remain unresolved, depends on two factors: (1) the substantive interrelationship between the resolved and unresolved issues, and (2) the comparative importance of the resolved and unresolved issues.

1. *Issue independence or dependence.* Suppose two salespersons argue heatedly with their supervisor over which one is entitled to the commission for a previous sale. The supervisor (mediator) can get them to implement their agreement not to make sarcastic remarks or berate one another during their forthcoming joint presentation to a new client, even though the compensation issue remains unresolved; the two matters are related but independent of one another. However, if the corporate president gets his division leaders to agree to decentralize the

company's personnel function among its twenty retail stores but fails to have them agree on a timetable for doing so, then, absent a direct order on the matter of timing, no one can implement that decentralization agreement because of the dependence of the resolved issue on the unresolved issue.

2. *Priority of issue.* Parties can reach agreement on issues that can be implemented independently of each other, but if the resolved issue is trivial and the unresolved matter important, then the parties have no incentive to implement their agreement. Suppose a government agency suddenly changes its program priorities and, as a result, immediately terminates its funding of those private agencies that no longer administer high-priority projects and reallocates their former budgets to those persons involved with high-priority endeavors. When the directors of the affected projects protest the action, the government agency then agrees to provide six months' notice to any agency whose funding might be cut as a result of a change in program priorities, but refuses to have that policy apply retroactively. That commitment for future action is of almost no value to the agencies that will lose their present funding and possibly go out of business. Thus, although it is accurate to state that the disputants have agreed on some matters that could be implemented, the value of their implementation is sharply reduced when considered in light of those issues that remain unresolved.

Forms of Agreement

Mediated agreements are either oral or written. Most terms of agreement are explicit, but some are deliberately vague. Some identify specific behavioral elements that parties agree to perform; others identify more general categories of behavior.

Whatever form the agreement takes, the mediator *must make certain people understand what it is that they are agreeing to.* If co-workers have resolved their dispute over who gets the corner office with the window, the mediator must make that explicit; if they have agreed to postpone a decision on that matter for three weeks, she must make that clear.

Written Agreements

A mediator can state terms of agreement in a variety of written formats. The most common form is a signed contract stating what each party promises to do. Other written formats for displaying the terms of agreement include press releases, memoranda of understanding between the parties; a letter from the mediator to the parties identifying what everyone has agreed to, written proposals exchanged between the parties and initialed by the negotiators and the mediator to reflect agreement on the various matters; or a straightforward change in the written statement of a particular policy, law, or practice that incorporates the terms of agreement.

There are obvious benefits to a written agreement. It makes the terms of agreement explicit and gives parties a chance to review their commitments before officially "signing off" on them. It prevents parties from adding or deleting obligations. It serves as a future reference for checking compliance. Finally, and not insignificantly, it represents to the parties the one tangible, concrete piece of evidence of their mutual success.

Writing the agreement is not a mop-up operation. In most contexts where a written agreement is appropriate, the mediator prepares a draft of the agreement. This enables her to exert control over the document's appearance, tone, and precision.

Appearance. A major component of the mediator's job is developing a logical order for discussing issues. In reducing the terms of agreement to writing, she must also choose the order in which they will be listed. Here are some guidelines:

1. Use a format that enables people quickly to find and read what their performance obligations are. This takes some imagination. If there are charts and graphs that detail the specific terms of agreement, summarize them in the body of the agreement but attach them as an appendix. If the agreement is long, develop a table of contents for it.

2. Make the document look official. Writing the agreement in pencil on the back of an envelope might produce a chuckle from U.S. history students, but it demeans the aura of importance that people want to attach to the resolution of their dispute. If possible, type it on clean paper and keep erasures to a minimum.

3. Begin with those items that entail a mutual obligation to act ("Smith and Jones agree not to make sarcastic remarks about each other during their joint presentation to new customers").

4. Insofar as possible, keep the agreement balanced. A mediator must not list twenty items that party A agrees to do for party B and then the five items that party B agrees to do for party A. Disperse them so that one party does not feel outmatched by the other, or rewrite them so the twenty items are reduced to five categories.

Tone. The agreement must state straightforwardly and clearly what each party agrees to do. A mediator must not encumber it with lengthy explanations of why the parties have adopted the various provisions. In some contexts, it is useful for the mediator to establish a positive context for the terms of agreement by developing a preface stating the general principles and goals to which the parties agreed when discussing the specific settlement terms. The language of the agreement must not be shrill or accusatory.

DON'T WRITE: Ellis agrees that her playing the record player at high volumes after 11:00 P.M. on Sunday through Thursday nights is rude and inconsiderate of Korman's rights and therefore agrees to wear earphones whenever she plays her record player after 11:00 P.M. on those nights.

WRITE: Ellis agrees to wear earphones whenever she plays her record player after 11:00 P.M. on Sunday through Thursday nights.

Precision. The mediator must use language that precisely captures what the parties have agreed to do. She must also make certain that deliberate ambiguities are precisely stated. Here are the most common traps to avoid:

1. *Names.* Use names rather than such jargon as "party of the first part." People need to know who has agreed to do what for whom.
2. *Pronouns.* Prounouns invite ambiguity, so minimize their use. Here is an excerpt from one agreement:

If Ms. T believes that Ms. K has not complied with the terms of this agreement, she will contact her through her attorney.

Is Ms. T to contact Ms. K by having Ms. T's attorney contact Ms. K., or is Ms. T supposed to contact Ms. K's attorney, who will relay the message to Ms. K? An agreement should not be an obstacle course. Make it clear.

3. *Abbreviations.* Even the most innocent of abbreviations can generate conflicting interpretations. If a tenant agrees on October 10, 1986, to vacate her apartment on 1/10/87, the landlord might think that her tenant will leave on January 10, 1987, whereas the tenant may believe she can stay until October 1, 1987. Since the written agreement will take precedence over any verbal understandings, a party will exploit the mediator's careless use of abbreviations to its maximum advantage.

4. *Methods of performance.* Some terms of agreement can be executed in more than one way. A mediator must persuade parties to perform their obligations in a manner that can be verified and is most likely to achieve full compliance. If one party agrees to return items by mail, the mediator must specify in the agreement that the person will get a receipt verifying the date she mailed them. Similarly, the mediator must write the agreement so that parties do not pay their debts with personal checks that bounce so high that one can dribble them to the bank!

5. *Evaluative terms.* What does it mean when someone promises to divide the toy trucks among the children "fairly," to repair the roof "satisfactorily," or to act "reasonably" or "in good faith"? These terms and phrases are meaningful concepts, but they are elastic in nature and do not identify *explicitly* those standards of performance against which one can evaluate contract compliance. A mediator must use such terms deliberately. If the parties agree that a "fair" division of toy trucks requires that every child have at least one toy, then the mediator must say so; if the roof repair is measured according to the subjective standard of being satisfactory to the owner rather than the more objective criterion of "meeting industry standards," she must make that explicit.

6. *Omissions or additions.* The mediator should write down *everything* that the parties have agreed to do, *and no more.* The mediator invites lasting hostility if, in the writing process, she mistakenly adds to or subtracts from the parties' verbal commitments.

7. *Admissions of wrongdoing.* A party may or may not admit wrongdoing as the basis for agreeing to perform in a certain way in the future. But such admissions have no place in a written agreement. A mediator must use precise but nonjudgmental language:

NOT: Joan Freeman agrees to pay Bob Lofton $150.00 in full payment for the bicycle that she *stole* from Lofton's son, Joe, on March 1, 1987.

BUT: Joan Freeman agrees to pay Bob Lofton $150.00 in full payment for the replacement of Joe Lofton's bicycle *that disappeared* on March 1, 1987.

8. *Misspellings.* Nothing is as offensive as seeing one's name misspelled in a formal written document. A mediator must record names and titles accurately.

9. *Pride of authorship.* The mediator must be prepared for the parties to criticize and alter the draft that she prepares for them. Her job is to capture their agreement in written format. But if the parties want to rewrite aspects of the agreement in language that is acceptable to them but different from what the mediator used, then the mediator should alter the language even if she believes that the substitute version is not as elegant or as sophisticated as her own.

The mediator cannot make the mistake of believing that her job is done when the parties have verbally agreed to a resolution of the issues. She must not relinquish the writing task—even if it is only a draft—to one of the parties. The person who writes the agreement establishes its format and creates its language; she photographs what the parties have agreed to do. If the mediator writes the agreement, then she can adopt a perspective consistent with her neutral posture.

The first draft, whoever writes it, becomes the focus of discussion. It is a rare person who will throw out an entire draft document and begin again; usually, people suggest alterations or modifications to the original draft. Thus, if one party prepares a draft of the agreement and submits it to the others for approval, that party will gain the upper hand in establishing its general appearance, tone, and precision. Of course, everyone must accept the written agreement before it becomes operative, so it does not serve a party's purpose to submit a draft agreement with language that is blatantly offensive to the others. But a party can gain the upper hand without being offensive; simply by agreeing to write the draft, for example, one party takes control of the discussion timetable. The mediator must make certain that parties do not lose their agreement in disputes over draftsmanship. The best way to do that is to take charge of the drafting process herself.

Nonwritten Agreements

In some contexts it is unnecessary or inappropriate to write down what the disputants have agreed to do. A person acting as a go-between among co-workers who are arguing over who should clean up the mess left in the photocopying room does not commit their agreement to writing—people just do what they have agreed to do. The same principle applies when a parent or guardian helps her children resolve a confrontation or a teacher resolves a dispute among two students who are fighting in her classroom.

Some disputes are resolved with a handshake; others conclude with an apology or a promise to behave in a certain manner in the future. Such informal resolutions do not mean that the disputes or their solutions are insignificant. A mediator cannot get caught in the trap of believing that important matters must be resolved in a written format while unimportant issues can be resolved otherwise.

Consider a typical employment situation in which one supervisor is uniformly despised by her subordinates because she uses offensive language, favors one employee when granting overtime work assignments, and disciplines some but not all employees for arriving late to work. During contract negotiations, the union proposes a series of demands that would stop these practices; because of the nature of collective bargaining, however, the union must propose rules that apply to *all* supervisors. An employer might acknowledge the legitimacy of the employees' concerns regarding the one supervisor but have reservations about adopting the proposed rules on a companywide basis. The resolution? The employer makes a verbal commitment to the union to fire the supervisor in exchange for the union withdrawing its proposal on this matter.

No employer or union would commit such an agreement to writing, for the employer wants to handle the discharge of its supervisor privately and on job-related grounds that are consistent with company and legal practices. But the employer is as much obliged, practically speaking, to do what she has orally agreed to do as she would be if she had reduced her commitment to writing, for failure to comply might result in the employees engaging in a job slowdown or wildcat strike.

Not putting things in writing permits people to comply with the terms of agreement while continuing to rant and rave. A mediator might be able to get the owner of a local television station and a civil rights organization to agree to a general plan for hiring more minority personnel in key corporate positions. Not committing that agreement to writing, however, enables the owner to condemn publicly all quota hiring systems as immoral and unconstitutional while she quietly but firmly acts according to the agreed-on affirmative action hiring program that, in content, bears a striking resemblance to the very systems she criticizes.

Just as a mediator cannot be lulled into the false belief that oral commitments are less important than written ones, so she must remember that actions speak louder than words; in the end, what people *do* to resolve their dispute is far more important than either what they say they will do to resolve it or what they pledge in writing to do. That observation is not meant to minimize the importance of written agreements nor to suggest that oral commitments are useless; rather, it is meant to put their value in some perspective. Ultimately, substance triumphs over form. At some point, people do what they are obliged to do not because they said or wrote that they would. Rather, they continue to honor their commitments, and the spirit of their commitments, because they conclude that their counterparts will continue to act as they have done. On the basis of the other party's performance, an individual or group develops confidence that others will not deliberately undercut their aspirations or interests. Thus a reciprocity of conduct takes hold. Thereafter, each party doesn't check a document every time she acts or canvass her memory bank to determine whether she is required to do what she contemplates doing; life is too rich and unpredictable for one to act with such an artificial straitjacket. One simply does what she believes to be warranted by or consistent with her commitments.

When discussions end, parties may feel hopeful and satisfied, but they don't always feel uplifted and renewed. The mediator's job is to make sure they do not leave feeling burdened and incapable of proceeding.

In the days to come, parties must place their dispute and its resolution in perspective. They must determine the priority they will continue to attach to it as they conduct their daily routine. They must deal with both its resolution and the consequences of the way in which they tried to resolve it.

The mediator's efforts and contributions to the discussion process are evaluated independently of the particular resolution the parties reach. A mediator has not failed if the parties do not successfully resolve all their negotiating issues. She *has* failed if she has not thoroughly canvassed and deployed every option at her command to facilitate a mutually acceptable outcome.

Part III
The Lessons
of Experience

12
Ethical Dilemmas and Practical Challenges

T he discussion of BADGER is now complete. Its portrayal makes clear why the mediator's role is so decisive in moving contending parties towards settlement. Its discussion illuminates the specific levers that mediators can use to propel parties toward agreement. It provides the basis for a mediator to act deliberately rather than by accident. While the BADGER guidelines and options are clear, how one combines them to generate a successful outcome varies with each situation; from the intervenor's perspective, then, no two situations are alike. As a result, he learns something new about himself and the process each time he serves. That is what makes mediating so rewarding.

Mediated discussion abounds in our daily lives, and its formal use is rapidly expanding. Conflict management is attracting many new participants. But with expansion and experimentation come concern and criticism of the nature of the service and the people who render it. Such healthy skepticism must be welcomed and addressed.

Particularly in settings where formal mediated discussions are the preferred method for resolving disputes, from neighborhood issues to controversies over the siting of toxic waste sites, certain types of questions, dilemmas, and challenges for the mediator frequently arise. A mediator must confront many of these challenges while on the firing line; he has very little time for contemplation—and he has only one chance to respond successfully. The stakes are high.

This chapter presents a number of these challenges in a question-and-answer format. Where appropriate, I cite personal experiences to illustrate the rationale for a particular answer.

1. *Can mediation begin only after the negotiating parties have tried and failed to resolve their dispute by themselves?*

Of course not. Mediation is a process for managing change. Disputants can anticipate differences of opinion and controversy. Using a mediator at the outset of their discussions can reduce strife, minimize problems, and establish a framework for dealing constructively with the challenges that arise.

> *Example.* In Connecticut, federal budget cuts in the early 1980s created enormous challenges for delivering social services to the state's elderly, homeless, disabled, and indigent populations. The budget for social services was slashed by 25 percent; categorical grants, however, were eliminated and replaced with a consolidated block grant—in essence, a state had less federal money to spend on social service programs, but it had the freedom to decide which programs it wanted to support and which to discontinue.
>
> In the first year, Connecticut officials and lawmakers reduced the budgets for all affected programs by 25 percent. But they were concerned. Such an across-the-board cut had a greater impact on small programs than on large ones. Some larger agencies could maintain programs by reallocating some fixed overhead costs to other program budgets or by minimizing services, but other agencies were effectively incapacitated. Social service priorities were being determined, then, not by human needs but by organizational structure. Officials wanted to have the budget allocations follow the planning process, rather than vice versa.
>
> With the governor's public support, the commissioners of the 18 affected state agencies, representatives for the 168 town and local governments, and spokespersons for the more than 800 nonprofit service providers throughout the state agreed to negotiate the issues of which social services should be preserved, what their relative priority should be, and what level of budgetary allocations they should receive. The parties selected me to serve as the mediator; my job was to help each team prepare for and conduct the negotiating sessions. Four months later, they signed an agreement.

We get the impression that we should use mediators only after parties have failed to resolve their dispute by themselves and only when the costs of their not settling it are dramatic. We read accounts of employers and union officials calling in a mediator at the eleventh hour of bargaining in an attempt to avert a strike. We see the U.S. secretary of state fly between England and Argentina in an attempt to help the parties achieve a settlement that will eliminate their felt need to fight a war in the Falklands. There are good reasons for using a mediator at that stage, but there is no compelling argument against using him at an earlier point in time.

2. *Should a mediator agree to serve if the parties have unequal bargaining power?*

It depends. This is a dangerously misleading question, and the mediator's response must be carefully crafted.

The concept of *bargaining power* is vague; even if one can catalog various sources of power—guns, numbers of people, information, principles, natural resources, religious faith, absence of competitors—no one can explicitly identify which source is most useful or how much of a particular source one must have in order to reach some threshhold level for "having power." It is even more treacherous, then, to assess whether the parties' bargaining power is *equal* or *unequal,* for doing so assumes we can measure all negotiating resources in some way and then use one standard to rank their relative effectiveness—that is, at best, a set of dubious assumptions.

Intuitively, however, we know that some people exert greater influence over others than vice versa. Favorite punching bag examples are big business gouging hapless workers, professors intimidating students, and worldly husbands imposing lopsided divorce settlements on helpless homemaker wives. These stereotypes do hint at real-world problems that arise from unequal distribution of resources.

The mediator operates in the reality that every bargaining situation involves persons with different bargaining power. Practically speaking, *different* bargaining power probably means *unequal* bargaining power. Before COMMITting oneself to serve as a mediator, a person must ask herself: Is the difference in bargaining power—economic, legal, experiential, political, or otherwise—so great that one party's conduct will dictate the outcome? If the answer is "yes," then she should not serve, for the discussion would proceed to a resolution whereby one party would never have to take into account the interests, needs, and aspirations of the others. Enshrining unilateral decision making in the legitimacy of collaborative problem solving is a sham that no mediator should endorse.

This response is good in theory, but it is difficult in practice for a potential mediator to know whether she confronts such a situation. How should she proceed?

A mediator must explore with the parties what has happened PRIOR-TO her entry. If the parties believe that mediated discussions represent their best option for securing their goals and each has an incentive to settle, then any doubts the mediator has about the potential unfavorable impact that will evolve from apparent disparities in bargaining power should be resolved in favor of respecting the parties' wishes to proceed.

There will always be doubts—and legitimate differences of opinion.

> *Example.* During the course of the mediated discussions in Connecticut involving the allocation of social service block grant monies to various program services, numerous observers commented to me that the representatives of the nonprofit agencies were inept as compared to their negotiating counterparts, that they had no leverage to force a change in program priorities, and that they were completely at the mercy of the state's negotiators in acquiring information necessary for making intelligent decisions; hence, they thought that I should stop the discussions or publicly announce that they were a sham. But I did not agree with that assessment; neither did the participants or their respective constituencies who ultimately approved the agreement. The fact that the terms of the final agreement dramatically changed the way in which decisions about social services delivery throughout the state would subsequently occur was an irony that these critics have not yet accepted.

The power disparities that make mediated discussions inappropriate are obvious because they are so blatant. A battered spouse should not engage in mediated discussions with the perpetrator without independent representation; a single, impoverished migrant worker who works a twelve-hour day and lives in squalid employee housing quarters will not secure his interests through mediated negotiations with his menacing foreman. The mediator does not apologize for the fact that mediation is a process for fostering independent decision making; if there are legitimate concerns that one party lacks the capacity to act independently (for fear of physical retaliation, inebriation, or minimal verbal or analytical skills), then she should prevent the process from going forward.

Sometimes these disparities do not appear until the parties are engaged in the discussions. What should the mediator do then? The answer is straightforward: stop participating, but exit without a public denunciation. The mediator simply informs the parties that in light of the way the discussions have progressed, she no longer believes she is able to serve them effectively—and she withdraws.

When the bargaining power differences are not so obvious as to cancel discussions, mediators will differ in their assessments of the facts and, therefore, whether or not to conduct discussions. There is room for honest differences of opinion. But a mediator must not confuse this decision about whether to proceed in light of bargaining disparities with the different matter of deciding whether to proceed on the basis that the likely outcome of the mediated discussions, given these differences in bargaining power, will not coincide with the mediator's preferred settlement terms. That issue is controversial and is raised directly by the next question.

3. From a mediator's perspective, is any agreement better than no agreement at all?

Definitely yes. But that response must not be misunderstood.

A mediator is an individual. He must decide, as do the negotiating parties, whether he will participate in mediated discussions. When he COMMITs himself to serve, he automatically answers the two questions that link the mediation process to our fundamental normative principles: he has reaffirmed his commitment to promoting equality of respect and concern, participatory decison making, and individual accountability; and he has concluded that using the mediation process to resolve this particular dispute will promote those values as well as any other alternative that is practically available.

If the individual mediator, or program designer contemplating the use of mediation, has any doubts about the desirability of resolving such controversies through mediated discussions, then he should resolve his differences before, not after, he has agreed to serve. For instance, suppose an individual employee wants to resolve his employment discrimination claim against his powerful employer through mediated discussions rather than by initiating a lawsuit. Should an individual agree to serve as a mediator? That individual has every right to determine whether his own commitment to eradicating discriminatory treatment is consistent with encouraging the private settlement of such individual charges. He must take into account the possibility that the employee might agree to settlement terms less favorable than those he would obtain if he were to prevail in his lawsuit; he must evaluate the benefits to the parties of expeditious settlement against the costs of those settlement terms not serving as a binding precedent for resolving future controversies. But once he makes that assessment and COMMITs himself to serve as mediator, his primary goal is to assist the parties reach a settlement on terms they find acceptable; only if he learns during the course of the mediated discussion that the parties are proposing terms that conflict with the fundamental values that supported the mediator's original commitment to serve should the mediator let his own preferences become decisive and bring the discussion to a close.

One must restate this point emphatically. It is not part of an individual's role *qua* mediator to question whether particular terms should be acceptable. It is irrelevant to the mediator if the terms of agreement are inefficient, shortsighted, or less than what one party could have gained in a winning lawsuit. What is relevant is that the parties have decided that, given their scheme of priorities, they can live with the solution, and the mediator is confident that the proposed terms will endure in practice. Given this basic understanding, if the parties ultimately determine that they would rather have no agreement at all than adopt any of the settlement terms they have considered during their discussion, that is fine. But the mediator's job, without apology, is to deploy every element of BADGER to facilitate a settlement; to him, any agreement is better than no agreement at all, for he would not COMMIT himself to serve if he thought that nonmediated outcomes were preferable to a potential settlement.

It is important to appreciate the difference between a mediator who does not participate in mediated discussions because he concludes that the difference in bargaining power among the parties is so skewed that one party is unable to participate competently in making joint decisions from the situation in which the mediator tries to stop the mediated discussions because the parties are about to accept settlement terms that the mediator personally disapproves of or believes fall short of meeting such laudable goals as efficiency, wisdom, or maximizing the general well-being of others. The former is appropriate; the latter oversteps the mediator's role.

4. Can a mediator be neutral?

Yes. The mediator must have no preference that particular negotiating issues be resolved one way rather than another. Consider the following range of negotiating issues:

A teachers' union and school district are deadlocked in their negotiations over whether the district can assign a teacher to more than two schools during the day, thereby necessitating multiple trips by the affected personnel.

A parent and fifteen-year-old son disagree about what time the son must return home following the school dance.

A social worker and youth counselor disagree over whether a child should be denied weekend visitation privileges with his family as a disciplinary measure for his having refused to eat his dinner at the institutional home.

It is certainly possible to find individuals capable of serving as mediators for these situations who have no preference that the matters be resolved one way rather than another. That is sufficient to meet the standard of neutrality.

The importance of remaining neutral cannot be overemphasized. If the mediator is not neutral, then one party will believe—correctly—that it is at an immediate disadvantage; the mediator and the other party are ganging up on her. That is not a formula for generating a successful resolution.

It is difficult to remain neutral. A mediator who sees an individual about to agree to terms that are less favorable than those she thinks she would win in court is particularly prone to steering discussions in one party's favor. People have great difficulty in letting others decide for themselves how they want to live, but paternalistic attitudes and pygmalion complexes are not consistent with effectively conducting mediated discussions.

One must not overstate the extent of one's neutrality. No one who has any ideas or principles will be neutral on every possible negotiating issue. People have definite convictions about educational programs, public safety policies, energy plans, social services, equal employment opportunity responsibilities, economic development options, and a host of other challenges that confront us in our personal and social environment. There is no reason to apologize for one's strong convictions; all one must acknowledge is that having such convictions disqualifies her from being a mediator in disputes involving those issues.

> *Example.* Suppose a group of terrorists disagree over which tactics to adopt to disrupt the Olympic Games. They search for a mediator to help them agree on an acceptable plan of attack. One hopes their search is fruitless. Why? Because we want people to condemn the very goal—destruction of innocent lives—that the terrorists want to achieve with a mediator's assistance.

An individual can lose her neutrality perceptually as well as substantively. For example, a parent who serves as a coach of a softball team on which her child plays may be accused of resolving controversies in a way that favors her child; the temptation to do so is certainly understandable. The reverse is often true as well: a parent, trying particularly hard not to be seen as playing favorites, may systematically ignore or undervalue her own child's interest or point of view. The lesson is simple: don't pretend to be a mediator in a situation in which one has a close personal or professional relationship with one of the parties.

Based on these comments about a mediator's neutrality, there is one obvious but important practical consequence to mention: since no one is neutral about all possible negotiating issues or negotiating parties, no one can plausibly represent herself as being able to mediate any dispute whatsoever.

5. *Should a mediator be active or passive?*

Neither. The question poses a false dichotomy. If a mediator does his job—BADGERs the parties—then his presence will make a difference. Whether he does it with histrionics or quietly is a matter of personal style, not strategy. When people envision an active mediator, they think of someone who throws out ideas for settlement, forces people to reconsider their positions, and prods people to settle. But that is what mediating is all about. What varies from dispute to dispute are the specific elements of CNTRL that a mediator deploys or the particular combination of techniques for generating movement that he adopts. How the mediator executes those aspects of his role is dictated not by whether he is active or passive but by the nature of the negotiating issues and the degree of rigidity in the parties' negotiating stance.

6. *Should a mediator identify "new" negotiating issues if the parties have not raised them themselves?*

No, unless doing so is necessary to make certain that the parties can implement their settlement terms or to help parties pass successfully from the more fluid, formative stage of their negotiation process to its more tangible, substantive component.

A mediator must not hesitate to identify additional matters that, if not addressed and resolved, will jeopardize compliance with the agreement. If Smith agrees to pay Jones $50 for the repair of Jones's bicycle that Smith damaged, but no one says anything about when or how the payment will be made, the mediator must raise those issues. Otherwise, compliance remains a hostage of those ambiguities.

If the mediator enters the discussions before the parties have developed or agreed to a formal agenda of negotiating issues, she can suggest additional issues for the parties to address if doing so will stabilize their negotiating relationship or expand their negotiating flexibility.

Example. A group of Native Americans took physical possession of a private campsite that was contiguous to the Adirondack

State Park in New York State. It demanded that the state grant
it clear legal title of the entire park; the state refused.

The parties existed in an uneasy alliance for months. State
police officers had multiple surveillance points around the
campsite; the occupants had twenty-four-hour guards pack-
ing guns. Legal charges of all sorts were thrown at the land
occupants, but no change resulted. Meanwhile, neighboring
residents had to pass the campsite going to and from a popular
lodge. One evening, a family left the lodge and drove past the
campsite on their way to town. A shot was fired. The bullet
traveled through the trunk of the car into the back seat and
hit a ten-year-old girl, who survived but was completely
paralyzed.

Fear mounted, rhetoric escalated, and demands for action increased. We intervened as mediators; the tension was
extraordinarily high. Rumors abounded; the day we arrived,
citizens told us they had heard reliable reports that a group
of four hundred armed Native Americans from South Dakota
had been seen passing through Chicago on their way to the
campsite in New York; twelve hours elapsed before the sheer
idiocy of that rumor was laid to rest. The citizens wanted the
Native Americans to leave; the Native Americans wanted title
to the land. County officials wanted to prosecute individuals
for a variety of criminal offenses, and politicians were clamor-
ing for action.

We proposed that the parties develop negotiating proposals addressed to the topic of establishing a rumor control mechanism. No one had previously identified this as an
agenda item for negotiation. No one pretended that it would
resolve the more substantive concerns, but everyone agreed
that the urgency of the situation demanded a short-term,
tangible, and effective device for minimizing miscalculations
and stabilizing various relationships. A procedure was promptly
negotiated.

7. *What if parties, during the mediated discussions, act in un-
cooperative or disruptive ways—interrupting, calling each other
names, or threatening acts of violence?*

A mediator must move quickly and decisively to quash such exchanges.

The basic principle guiding the mediator's response to such behavior is straightforward: mediation requires everyone to agree to the outcome. The use of abusive language is personally offensive and disrespectful; pragmatically speaking, it generates a defensive response from those at whom it is directed, thereby making accommodation much more difficult to achieve. Using words like "slumlords," "pigs," and "welfare bums" inflame reactions rather than gain cooperation. Threats of violence obviously do the same thing.

If parties malign each other's character, the mediator simply directs them to address each other by name or title. If someone threatens violence, the mediator declares a caucus and meets first with that party; he forcefully tells the party that either he will terminate his threats of violence and engage in mediated discussions, or the mediator will stop the discussions with the explicit statement to everyone that that party's threats to commit acts of violence undermine the integrity of any possible agreement and make it useless for people to continue talking.

A mediator must be patient, nondefensive, and willing to be the scapegoat of the parties' vehemence and tirades. But the types of conduct noted here don't simply challenge the mediator's good will; they are direct attacks on the principles that support the use of mediated discussions. The mediator, as the guardian of the process, must do that which enables it to proceed. If the parties do not want to act within its basic structure, then the mediator must protect both his own dignity and the integrity of the process by bringing the discussion to a halt.

8. *What if parties ask the mediator for her assessment of whether a particular offer of settlement is fair or reasonable?*

Don't give it. A party always tries to get the mediator to support its viewpoint; it tries to get the mediator to agree that its proposal is fair or reasonble or that it is acting "in good faith." The mediator must resist all such attempts by a party to gain her endorsement of its behavior. Consider the consequences.

If the mediator agrees that a party's offer is "reasonable"—for instance, that the employer's offer to increase wages by an amount equal to the cost of living is "reasonable"—then any proposal that exceeds that figure will automatically be labeled "unreasonable." But no longer is it simply the employer alone who believes that the union's proposal to increase wages by 6 percent is "unreasonable" when the cost of living has increased by less than 4 percent; now, the employer can gloat, even the "impartial, objective" mediator believes that figure is "off the wall."

The mediator's response to such endorsement requests must be prompt and uniform. She must put the responsibility right back in the parties' laps. Her response would be: "It is not important whether I believe the proposal is reasonable. The question is whether it is an arrangement that the two of you can live with."

There may come a time, however, when the parties are completely frustrated and want the mediator's best judgment as to what the settlement terms should be.

9. Should a mediator ever make a formal "mediator's proposal" for settlement?

Yes, but only if he is asked to do so by all parties to the dispute and only after he has exhausted all attempts to identify possible settlement terms and persuade parties to adopt them.

A mediator's proposal is his formal recommendation, indicating how he believes all unresolved issues should be settled. The goal of such a proposal is to recommend terms that the parties will accept. If the proposal is successful, parties adopt the recommendations as a package and a resolution is secured.

When the mediator makes his proposal, he is not stating what he personally believes is a "fair" or "reasonable" resolution of the particular matters. Rather, he takes what he has learned from the parties in their joint sessions and caucuses; considers their respective needs, interests, and constraints; and proposes specific settlement terms that he believes the parties will accept. The mediator does not try to act as a judge by determining the rights and duties of the respective parties, nor does he try to split everything in half. Instead, the mediator tries to shape a future relationship for the parties that is workable and responsive to their most important interests and concerns.

The mediator must recognize that, once he has made his proposal, his usefulness to the parties will be severely restricted, if not completely nullified. If the parties accept the proposal, fine; if they alter only limited aspects of it, the mediator can help them do so. But if the parties do not adopt his major recommendations or a substantial number of them, then they will not trust his subsequent efforts to help them reach an agreement, for they will justifiably believe him to be an advocate for his own proposals rather than a neutral intervenor. Given that reality, a mediator makes a formal settlement proposal only after he has badgered the parties to explore all other avenues for settlement.

A mediator resists the request to make formal settlement proposals for very practical reasons. First, parties often ask for the mediator's assessment early in the discussions; to give it to them at that point short-circuits the negotiation process, undermines the principle that parties must take responsibility for resolving their disputes, and puts the mediator in the posture of making recommendations that are not grounded in an enriched understanding of the parties' interests and history. Second, advice is cheap, but helping people resolve their concerns requires effort. If the mediator's effort to help others resolve their dispute is to succeed, then he must become immersed in the dynamics of the dispute and engaged in the discussion and settlement-building process; offering solutions too quickly converts a mediator into a consultant. Finally, people tend to comply with the settlement terms, and to respect their negotiating counterparts, if they have played a meaningful role in developing them. Having to live according to terms that an outsider has proposed can be a constant irritant to one's sense of independence.

The one context in which the mediator's formal proposal is very useful and certain to be adopted is when his proposal simply recommends settlement terms that the parties have privately indicated to him they will accept. Sometimes the parties need a scapegoat or punching bag in order to settle; they need to advise their constituents that they agreed to proposals advanced by a neutral party but did not cave in to their counterpart's proposal. The mediator's formal proposal satisfies that need perfectly.

10. *What does a mediator do if the parties have reached impasse?*

She forces them to examine the costs of not settling. If non-mediated options appear more attractive to one or more parties than any solutions being considered at that time, there will be no settlement and the discussions will terminate.

That may seem too easy a response to such an important challenge. But the response is correct; it is the challenge that has been miscast.

The crucial assessment that the mediator must make is not what strategy the mediator should employ if the parties reach impasse but, rather, how she can determine *if* the parties have reached an impasse.

Our conventional image of people at an impasse is that they are deadlocked on some matters. They have exchanged proposals and ideas, perhaps even made some compromises, but now they refuse to budge from their announced positions. They may play brinksmanship with each other or break off discussions and pursue independent courses of action to protect their interests.

This conventional image of impasse is misleading. Instead, the mediator must view the concept of impasse as a continuum. An impasse does not exist simply because people have proposed incompatible solutions to various negotiating issues. Otherwise, parties would reach impasse the moment they offered different solutions to the various issues in dispute. The key criterion for determining whether impasse exists is the degree to which a party is committed to pursuing nonnegotiated solutions if its preferred solution is not adopted.

Looking at the concept of impasse from this perspective generates two conclusions: first, in some contexts, parties can reach impasse very rapidly; second, the greater one party's need to secure the other's cooperation in order to achieve its own goals—the more they are "married" to one another—the less likely it is that they will ever really reach an impasse (even if they claim to be at that point).

Consider the following examples.

Example 1. Shaw, a recent recipient of an MBA degree, wants to pursue a career in human resource management. She interviews with Siskin for an entry-level personnel position in a large, well-known department store. Two weeks later, Siskin telephones Shaw and offers her a position; the annual salary is $15,000, and the position requires that she work every weekend. Shaw decides to negotiate. She indicates to Siskin that she can accept the position only if the beginning salary is $19,000 and she does not have to work on weekends. Siskin counters by stating that her bottom line is a starting salary of $15,500 and a promise to consider changing Shaw's schedule after six months of employment. Shaw responds that she cannot take the job for a salary less than $17,500. Siskin reacts by withdrawing the job offer and hanging up.

Example 2. A school board engages in negotiations with the teachers' union; there are seven hundred teachers in the public school system, which serves ten thousand students. The school board proposes a salary increase of 5 percent for each year of a two-year contract and demands that the individual teacher pay the entire amount of any future premium increases in the health insurance plan; the union counters by proposing a 9.5 percent salary increase for each year of a two-year contract, an expansion of employer-paid health insurance benefits to include dental coverage, and an increase in the number of teachers who can take sabbatical leave from the current level of three teachers per year to a new maximum of seven teachers per year. Six months later, neither party has modified any of its proposals; their present contract is about to expire. Both parties declare that they have reached an impasse.

In example 1, the employer and the job candidate quickly reached an impasse. Shaw decided that the employer's last offer was not sufficiently attractive and chose to pursue other options. Had a mediator been present, she would have caucused with Shaw and forced her to consider the consequences of not reducing her salary demands: the time she would spend looking elsewhere for employment; the lost opportunity to acquire competent training and pursue a well-defined career track in an established, reputable company; and the like. If Shaw believed she could do better elsewhere, she would reject the mediator's attack and simply continue her job search.

This type of transaction is a typical event in our daily lives. We often reach impasse over some issue—usually money—and quickly move on. We don't pursue the discussion because we believe we can get what we want elsewhere. But if what we are seeking is scarce and only our negotiating counterpart can provide it to us, then our mobility is restricted. We must find a way to gain a settlement.

That is the dynamic operating in the second example. The parties claim they are at impasse, but they really are not. They may be stuck; they may break off discussions for a while. But what are their options to reaching settlement? The board cannot close down the school system, as a private employer might close down his business. And unlike an individual conducting a job search, the teachers cannot leave en masse to work for another employer. In a very practical sense, the parties must reach an agreement. That does not mean, of course, that the process of doing so may not be strewn with grief, anger, harsh words, work stoppages, and the like. Ultimately, however, the parties must strike a deal.

A mediator analyzes two elements when assessing whether the parties have reached impasse. First, she examines whether the parties have a relationship such that nonnegotiated solutions are a practical alternative. Second, she examines the parties' stated and unstated positions to see whether she can detect any flexibility in their positions.

The mediator wants to analyze the parties' relationship to determine their relative degree of interdependence; the higher it is, the less likely that they will reach impasse. Parties do not need to be "married" to each other in order for their relationship at a particular time to be such that they have no practical alternative to working out an acceptable solution. Two co-workers may detest each other; each might be looking elsewhere for employment. But if neither can afford to be unemployed and each wants to continue to receive favorable performance reviews, then their supervisor should be able to badger them into finding a way to overcome their "incompatible work styles" and complete the assignment that requires their working together.

The stronger the interdependence among the parties, the more susceptible they are to being persuaded to find an acceptable resolution. That should prod the mediator to redouble her efforts to generate movement from the parties. She has an arsenal of persuasive techniques at her disposal, and she must try them repeatedly. She must probe for the slightest hint of flexibility by reexamining the parties' stated and unstated priorities, reviewing the facts and their ambiguities, studying the language in which proposed settlement terms are couched, and monitoring the rate and extent of concessions and counter offers that the parties have made. Before appealing to the costs of not settling, the mediator must be certain she has accurately read each party's movements and appreciates its constraints. She must not hesitate to acknowledge an impasse if it arises, but, more than anyone else, she must not do so precipitously. The parties and observers quickly become discouraged by apparently clashing, immobilized public positions; the mediator must be more subtle and persistent.

> *Example 3.* In the tripartite mediated discussions conducted in Connecticut, the three parties—the state agencies, the non-profit service providers, and local government representatives— reached tentative agreement on the priority ranking of the various social services funded by the $33.1 million social service block grant. That agreement was contingent on the parties agreeing to the funding level of the various services, with the allocation to one particular service being the bellwether. In separate caucuses, the local government team proposed that the bellwether service be funded at a level exceeding $2 million; the state government representative and nonprofit spokespersons indicated that their teams would consider funding it in the $60,000–70,000 range. I indicated to each party separately that there was an "enormous" difference in their proposed figures. Eager to preserve the momentum generated by the tentative agreement on the priority ranking of the services, I proposed that the parties accept the proposed service priority rankings and commit themselves to allocating a "substantial" amount of money to the bellwether service; everyone accepted that framework and agreed to negotiate the specific dollar allocations for all the services at the next meeting, scheduled to occur in two weeks.
>
> During that two-week interval, I talked with state government representatives and tried to prod them to allocate a meaningful amount of dollars to that bellwether service. Meeting its commitment to me to do so, the state's spokesperson opened the discussion of budget allocations at the next meeting by proposing to allocate $250,000 to the bellwether service. It was 11:00 A.M. The offer was accepted by the nonprofit team but adamantly rejected by the local government team, which demanded that $2 million be given to support the service.

I declared a caucus and met separately with the parties to discuss the various allocations to all the services. There was no concession on the bellwether service. The state team met by itself. At 4:00 P.M. it made a new offer, prefacing it by stating that this was the state's "final" offer, to be treated on a take-it-or-leave-it basis. The state now offered to grant $500,000 to the bellwether service.

The same scenario followed. The nonprofit team immediately accepted the offer, but the local government team, to the utter astonishment of the state's negotiating committee, soundly rejected it as inadequate. I turned to my colleagues on the mediation team and predicted that we would have an agreement by midnight, with some amount less than $1 million being granted to the contested service.

At 8:00 P.M., after nine hours of continuous discussions and no universal acceptance of the $500,000 offer, one member of the state team approached me and heatedly demanded to know when I was going to "start mediating." To him, of course, "mediating" meant getting the local government team to accept the state's "final" offer. I told him I would start mediating as soon as the state team stopped dictating its demands to others and started negotiating. Startled, he muttered a reply and left.

At 8:45 P.M., a member of the negotiating team for the nonprofit agencies sent me a note imploring me to recess the discussions until the next day, when the more "reasonable" persons on the local government team would rejoin the talks. I responded that since the people on that team who had the power to make decisions were present, there was no need to adjourn. Spectators in the audience were mingling in and out. There was a sense that everyone was stuck in an intractable rut. I was confident that the difference was not in the dollars, but I could not think of a new tactic that would persuade the local government team to move off its $2 million demand.

Suddenly, one member of the nonprofit agencies' negotiating team stated that he thought the state's proposal of $500,000 for this service would be the maximum the state legislature would approve when deciding whether to adopt the tripartite agreement as part of its final budget. Instantly I knew that this was the line of argument that would succeed. Before the local government team could reply, I immediately called for a caucus. At 9:30 P.M. all parties agreed to an allocation formula that provided a minimum of $500,000 and, under certain conditions, a maximum of $750,000 to the bellwether service.

Why was I so confident that the parties had not truly reached impasse but would, in fact, settle? First, I was confident that the nonprofit team would accept whatever the state proposed to allocate to the bellwether service, for the state had never increased its offer for the bellwether service by taking dollars away from the priority services of the nonprofit agencies; as long as that formula remained consistent, the challenge would be reduced to convincing only one team—the local governments—to move toward settlement.

Second, the state's rhetoric about "final offer" and "take it or leave it" is just that. No mediator ever feels constrained by such talk. The real question is whether a party is likely to pursue nonnegotiated avenues to achieve its objective if the other party does not accept its last proposal; if that seems likely, then—and only then—does characterizing the offer as final have some significance. We were nowhere near that point. Everyone needed each other's support to make sensitive and controversial budget decisions; despite the histrionics, no one was going to walk away. Finally, and most important, the state's progression of offers indicated both substantial movement and significant room for more. In less than two weeks' time, the state had increased its proposal by more than 300 percent—from $70,000 to $250,000. Between 11:00 P.M. and 4:00 P.M., it increased its offer by 100 percent—from $250,000 to $500,000. There was no way I would let the state freeze its position after such an enormous increase. I did not think I could get it to double its offer to $1 million; but anything less than another 100 percent increase— anything less than $1 million—I thought was fair game.

So, while individual negotiators and public observers became openly exasperated at what appeared to be an impregnable impasse, I was confident that we were not even close to one. It was a good lesson not only in the value of persistence but also in the need for a mediator to evaluate a party's flexibility or rigidity on the impasse issue in the context of its overall negotiating behavior.

11. *What should the mediator do if he learns, as a result of caucusing with the parties, that there is overlap in what the parties are willing to settle on?*

Use that knowledge to get a settlement. The ethical dilemma is more apparent than real.

This challenge arises only because the mediator chose to caucus. Suppose a landlord tells the mediator in caucus that he would accept $100 for settlement of the rent arrears rather than the $300 he has been demanding; then, when the mediator caucuses with the tenant, the tenant volunteers to pay $150 in order to settle the matter. Only the mediator knows about this $50 overlap. What should he do?

He must immediately realize that he has been given leverage for gaining settlement on any outstanding unresolved issues. For instance, if the landlord refuses to fix the tenant's stove until he receives payment for the rent due, the mediator might persuade him to fix the appliance immediately in return for getting more than $100 from the tenant. The mediator can pursue that line of inquiry because he knows he has some resources with which to work.

When the only unresolved issue is payment of rent arrears, the mediator faces a dilemma: he will determine who gets the $50 windfall by deciding which party speaks first when they reconvene. Whichever party he asks to speak first will forfeit $50. The easiest way to avoid the dilemma is for the mediator to bring the parties together, mention that in private discussions each had indicated a willingness to settle at figures that were mutually acceptable, and then suggest that they settle on the sum of $125 to resolve the issue of rent arrears. If a mediator finds this approach too manipulative, he can simply reconvene the parties, remind them that all other issues have been resolved, and indicate that there is an agreement in principle on how to solve the one remaining item; then, assuming he has obtained the parties' permission to do so, the mediator tells them what each is willing to do about the rent arrears and lets them resolve the difference themselves.

12. *What is face saving?*

Face saving refers to either procedural or substantive matters that, if handled in a particular way, enable the parties to the dispute to maintain their personal dignity and reputation both with each other and among their peers. Face-saving matters are integral to the overall settlement arrangement because they make the rest of the terms palatable or acceptable.

Face saving is not a sham. A mediator should not minimize its importance. Various needs give rise to face-saving concerns: the need to appear strong to one's constituents, to maintain a certain relationship with one's negotiating counterpart, or to retain a level of personal dignity. How do these needs materialize in practice?

Consider the school situation mentioned previously. Suppose that elected school board members are inundated with telephone calls from taxpayers who criticize as exorbitant the board's offer of a 5 percent salary increase for its teachers. The teachers' union, however, demands that its negotiating committee not waiver from its proposed 9.5 percent increase. The board and the teachers' union ask the mediator to make a formal mediator's proposal. Both know the recommendation will be 8 percent and both are prepared to accept it. Both will publicly berate the mediator for making such a recommendation and then, in the interests of getting an agreement, will accept her proposal.

Similarly, a mediator might, in a caucus, persuade a parent to agree to let her child stay out with friends until 1:00 A.M. on a weekend night; the parent had been insisting that the child return home by 11:00 P.M. The parent does not want her child to have the impression that the mediator forced her into agreeing to that arrangement or that, by agreeing to this, the parent no longer intends to exercise parental control over her child. The face-saving way to allow the parent to agree to the arrangement while satisfying her desire not to have her respect or authority undercut by the mediator is to have the parent tell the child what she is now willing to do.

What constitutes an acceptable face-saving arrangement is dominated by a party's sense of herself. That makes face saving just one more dimension of mediated discussions that is dramatically affected by the individuals who are involved in it.

13. *How firm and detailed must mediated agreements be?*

The need for precision varies with the situation. The mediator must not paralyze the parties from acting by insisting on a phantom certainty.

Most people think that when parties agree on certain matters, everyone knows what has been "offered" and "accepted." A negotiated agreement, however, is more fluid than that image suggests. Some terms of agreement are constitutionally vague: neighbors agree not to "harass" each other; parents agree to "respect" their teenager's privacy; teachers agree to develop a make-up exam that will "fairly" test a student's knowledge of the subject matter and will be "no more difficult" than the exam originally given; employers agree to terminate employees only if there is "just cause." What have these people actually agreed to do? These terms and concepts are not meaningless, but they are subject to varying, and conflicting, interpretations. A mediator must not block such terms of agreement simply because they are vague; they may be as precise as the subject matter allows, or their use may reflect a deliberate decision by the parties to postpone their attempts to agree on a more precise meaning.

Some oral commitments consist of a simple assertion: "Don't worry—I'll take care of that in my own way." Any party who accepts such a representation is trusting the speaker to respond to the situation without knowing exactly what the speaker will do. Unless the mediator believes such uncertainty jeopardizes compliance with the agreement, he should not be disturbed by the fact that there is not one explicit solution corresponding to each formulated issue; the absence of logical symmetry need not diminish the integrity of the agreement.

Some persons insist on certain terms of agreement as a face-saving measure, knowing even when they make the demand that subsequent events will render compliance with such terms infeasible. Divorcing spouses might insist on a provision that guarantees their infant children the right to choose their custodial parent upon reaching the age of fifteen. But if the children's schooling, friends, and related activities for ten years will center around the environment of one custodial parent, then the likelihood that the children will "really" make such a choice is minimal; the noncustodial parent realizes this, will not contest it when it occurs, but insists on including such a provision so that he or she can assure the children that neither parent ever abandoned them.

A mediator cannot fall into the trap of believing—and then insisting—that a mediated agreement must embody a detailed plan of action that anticipates and makes provision for resolving all future contingencies. To assess an agreement against such a standard is to grasp for certainty in an uncertain world. A mediated agreement must be developed with an appreciation for the diversity and unpredictability of life's experiences; that means some aspects of it will simply be a road map for future action, rather than a finely detailed understanding.

Acknowledging the role and value of ambiguities and uncertainties is not to excuse sloppiness when precision is possible. It does, however, prevent us from being lulled into the false belief that reaching an agreement automatically entails a problem-free future.

14. *Should a mediator agree to assume a formal role in the implementation of the agreement if the parties so request?*

Where possible, no. A mediator must be a catalyst in spurring parties to reach agreement; she must not be an ever-present crutch for them.

Four problems arise when a mediator assumes an integral role in the implementation of the settlement. First, if the parties want the mediator to remain neutral during the implementation stage, then that means the parties want the mediator to be a compliance officer, always checking to make sure all parties have done what they said they would do. Making the transition from a facilitating posture to a monitoring role is not as easy as one might suspect; one problem is that the parties themselves, because of their involvement with that mediator during the process of developing the agreement, do not view her as the authoritative figure that the role of compliance officer requires.

Second, if the people responsible for implementing the agreement are the same ones who participated in developing it, there is a tendency for the parties to continually rehash with "their" mediator what transpired during the mediated discussions. Focusing on the past rather than the future can impede the effective implementation of the agreement.

Third, a mediator can be unnecessarily cautious in executing her BADGER role if she knows she will participate in implementing the agreement. A mediator must not hesitate to persuade, cajole, push, prod, or provoke parties into an agreement; she must take risks in order to get a settlement. She cannot constrain her efforts for fear that she will undermine her effectiveness during the implementation phase. A mediator is not irreplaceable; someone else, if necessary, can help the parties live with their agreement.

Fourth, sometimes the people who implement the agreement are *not* the same ones who participated in the mediated discussions. This is typically the case when representatives of an employer and a union develop an agreement that personnel at the building or local level are responsible for implementing. It also occurs when leaders of a community organization negotiate with officials of a private corporation to establish a summer employment program for minority youths, and lower-echelon personnel from both organizations are charged with implementing the program. These new players need to develop their own dynamics of interaction; they need to take command of the terms of agreement and operate with a shared understanding of their meaning. If the mediator is put into the position of being the expert who can clarify the original intent of a particular term or clause, that developing synergy is disrupted and the mediator is converted from a badger to an umpire.

There is, of course, another way in which the mediator might be asked to participate in implementing the agreement: the parties might ask the mediator to participate because she has the requisite expertise that the parties have agreed to obtain as part of their agreement. Suppose the parties to the mediated discussion agree to secure the services of an investment counselor to help them analyze their portfolio; presume also that the person serving as the mediator is a professional investment counselor. The parties trust her and ask her to be the investment counselor that they are committed to obtaining. Should she agree to serve? Absolutely not. No one is indispensable. The mediator may be the acknowledged expert in her field of endeavor. If she chooses to serve as a mediator, however, she must not use that role as a conduit for obtaining other business. Otherwise, no party could ever be certain that a mediator was prodding them toward settlement terms that matched *their* priorities rather than the mediator's personal needs.

15. *Must all mediated discussions take place in private rather than being open to public observation?*

No.

This is a controversial position. Most people maintain that mediated discussions must be conducted in private so that parties can aggressively engage in the settlement-building process without feeling inhibited by a curious crowd or being deterred by reactions to selective public reports of their conduct.

The contexts that people think of when arguing for the need for such privacy are collective bargaining sessions between employers and unions in the private or public sectors, and international negotiations of various kinds. There are strong arguments to be made for conducting such discussions away from a viewing public:

There may be competitive or confidential information that cannot be discussed publicly but must be shared in order for parties to appreciate the constraints under which everyone is operating.

If the agreement requires approval by a negotiator's constituency, then the negotiator wants to present the tentative agreement to his membership in the manner he believes most conducive to reasoned debate and careful deliberation. But if various aspects of the agreement are reported publicly before such a presentation is made, he loses the chance to set the context for the ensuing debate.

If aspects of the agreement are publicly reported as being settled, and a party's constituency is upset by those terms, it may force its negotiating team to adopt a more rigid posture on the remaining items as a way of retaliating for the earlier concessions.

Discussions, by their very nature, must be fluid, with some items being resolved only tentatively until others are definitively settled; public reporting of "agreements," often neglects that distinction and forces the negotiators to explain why certain "agreements" no longer exist.

Conducting mediated discussions in public encourages nonproductive histrionics and speech making by the parties, reduces all discussions in public to a "report" of each party's present position, and removes the "real mediating and negotiating" to the back rooms and telephones.

These are important insights, but their universal applicability, not to mention their accuracy, can be legitimately challenged. Mediation is used in a variety of contexts. In situations involving a limited number of disputants arguing over interpersonal matters—problems among neighbors, students, co-workers, consumers and merchants, and the like—the arguments for privacy lose their force. There is no constituency who must approve the parties' settlement, so worries about adverse constituent reaction to public reporting miss the mark. Although some disputes involve confidential information and may best be handled in private (for example, disputes involving performance appraisals or salary data, although a growing body of management literature questions the wisdom of maintaining privacy even in this domain), the remainder could be conducted in public view; it is certainly not self-evident that disputes involving charges of sexual harassment at the workplace, for example, should not be discussed in the "public" of that office environment. Concerns that grandstanding to an audience will generate public support for a particular outcome are not compelling; in these types of disputes the parties themselves have almost complete control over the outcome. Finally, to favor private discussions in order to protect an individual's reputation from harm presumes that decent people never become embroiled in controversy; there is no reason to believe that, much less enshrine it in the operating procedures of mediated discussions.

For mediated discussions involving such public issues as reducing budget allocations to particular services, permitting industrial development on or near public park lands, or siting toxic waste disposal plants, there are compelling reasons to support a presumption in favor of conducting them in public. Parties are capable of discussing both trivial and complicated issues in public. Having the discussions open to public observation can provide an incentive for parties to prepare thoroughly and conduct themselves in an exemplary fashion; contrary to the expressed concern that negotiators will grandstand for their constituencies, parties do not want to embarrass themselves by appearing poorly prepared, uninformed, obstinate, or unreasonable. The public nature of the proceeding forces parties to depersonalize their comments, more so than in private exchanges; this in itself contributes to the settlement-building process. If members of a negotiating team need time to talk among themselves, they can always conduct private caucuses; but citizens should witness how the results of those deliberations are incorporated into the ensuing discussions so that they are confident that caucuses do not become merely an avenue for parties to avoid public accountability.

Conducting mediated discussions in a public forum is comparable to conducting courtroom trials in open session. The public—whether defined in a given setting as the family, the corporate entity, or the community at large—should have the right to observe what transpires in mediated discussions and to evaluate the issues in dispute, the quality of their resolution, and the manner in which all participants— parties and mediator alike—operate. These processes must not be shrouded in mystery. If the public does not understand why the participants in mediated discussions do the things they do, that only underscores the need for more public education about the dynamics of those processes and more public access to them. There are compelling arguments for restricting some sessions, or some types of mediated discussions, from public view. But those occasions should be the exception, not the rule. In a democratic society, the presumption should favor an open forum.

16. Should professional mediators be licensed?

No, but they must be trained.

All of us act as mediators in our roles as parent, friend, supervisor, co-worker, teacher, neighbor, and citizen. Life demands it. Requiring everyone to have a license to do so is as silly as requiring a license to cook or spell; people must perform these activities as best they can in order to get from day to day—they cannot simply abstain until they have been properly certified. That does not mean that we cannot all improve our skills. But *training* a person to serve as a mediator must be sharply distinguished from *licensing* that person to act as one.

For some people, mediating is their vocation. Professional mediators may be employees of government agencies who mediate labor–management collective bargaining sessions or public policy controversies. Some resolve controversies involving prisoner grievances, parent dissatisfaction with education programs for disabled children, or consumer complaints. Some professionals specialize in mediating divorce cases; others handle only disputes involving charges of employment discrimination. Two distinct, but related, questions arise: Can a person who capably mediates some of these disputes transfer her process skills so as to mediate effectively all these different kinds of cases? Should persons be licensed in order to serve as mediators for some or all of these types of disputes?

An effective mediator is more than simply a process expert; she must also be knowledgeable about the subject matter of the dispute. We examined this subject when identifying the desirable traits of a mediator. A person cannot be sensitive to a party's constraints, for instance, if she knows nothing about the party's history or the context in which the dispute arose. Anyone who wants to mediate a divorce case but knows nothing about tax law will be unaware of the multiple leverage points that are available for generating flexibility. The person who tries to resolve a controversy between an unhappy homeowner and a roofing company but is not familiar with the intricacies of roofing construction or the realities of operating a business cannot distinguish viable solutions from pipe dreams. Being a process expert is not a sufficient condition for being an effective mediator.

The question then arises: What subject matters must a mediator be knowledgeable about? To understand and execute the basic elements of BADGER requires her to have an analytical understanding of such concepts as power, trust, representation, and compromise, as well as an appreciation of motivation and communication theory. To that she must add an understanding of the various dimensions of the subject matter in dispute. But it is not reasonable to expect one individual to be conversant in all matters that bear upon the subject matter in dispute; one dispute—for instance, between tobacco industry representatives and government health officials—might require expertise in such diverse areas as political theory and operations, law, economics, psychology, accounting, advertising, chemistry, biology, computer science, and history. No one can be an expert in all these matters, nor is such expertise necessary in order to mediate effectively. Being knowledgeable in some of these areas, however, is essential for being an effective mediator; the areas of expertise that are most useful should be left to the parties to decide when they select their mediator.

The argument for licensing persons to serve as mediators, if compelling at all, must have a limited focus; it must apply only to those persons who want to serve as mediators for disputes that regularly arise in discretely identifiable subject matter areas. Prime candidates for consideration include mediation in such law-based areas as divorce and employment discrimination and in such industry-based settings as real estate transactions and building construction. Does it make sense to impose licensing requirements on those who mediate disputes in these relatively narrowly defined areas?

One can make a compelling case for requiring mediators to develop a knowledge of the concepts, principles, practices, and rules that are germane to these particular areas of dispute. But how one develops that knowledge base must not be artificially circumscribed. Licensing procedures not only restrict entry into a particular service, but are often tied to requiring the candidate to be trained in a certain way—for example, by obtaining a degree in an accredited college or graduate program. Mediation is far too diverse and fertile a field to benefit from such restrictions, at least at present. By attending various seminars and educational programs sponsored by professional associations, trade organizations, or universities, a person wanting to mediate these subject-specific cases can study and master the relevant material.

But the subject matter cannot be examined in isolation from the way mediators use such information to help parties move toward agreement. Various mediation agencies, consulting firms, and professional and trade organizations must be far more diligent than they currently are in incorporating subject-specific rules, information, and cases into their training programs for mediators. They must carefully blend subject and process in order to teach someone how to effectively BADGER parties to resolve particular types of disputes. Regrettably, present training and education efforts typically reinforce rather than demolish the separation between *process skills* and *content knowledge*, with mediation agencies and consultants emphasizing process skills divorced from particular subject areas, and professional and trade organizations conducting seminars on subject-related developments, oblivious to the specific ways a mediator might find such information useful.

One cannot become a skilled mediator by attending a two-hour orientation session or by mediating case after case without systematically analyzing what one has done. What is needed is a comprehensive plan for training professional mediators. There must be various levels of mediator training—beginning, intermediate, and advanced—for disputes ranging in content and complexity from interpersonal problems among neighbors to multiparty business or political controversies. Until this happens, efforts to provide the requisite process and substantive training will remain uneven and episodic, and those persons who want to acquire or improve their skills as mediators in a given subject area will have to design their own course of study and training. It is this pedagogical vacuum that sustains misguided calls for licensing procedures.

Demands for licensing procedures, even restricted to the most focused subject-matter areas, are premature; at present, the market system is a far better screening mechanism for protecting the public from charlatans than is any pseudoprofessional attempt at regulation. But the absence of systematic, substantive mediator training materials and programs that serve a diversity of persons and subjects should no longer be tolerated.

13
Conclusion

Mediators frequently jest that they wish they were half as good at solving their own disputes as they are at helping other people resolve their controversies. That offhand comment contains several kernels of truth.

The first and most obvious point is that it is difficult for anyone to be objective, imaginative, patient, and thoughtful when he is enmeshed in a controversy in which he has a decided stake in the outcome. The sting of the comment derives from the realization that it is in precisely those situations that the mediator's characteristics, skills, and strategies are most valuable.

We often use mediating skills and strategies even when we are not assuming a mediator's role. When we try to make a sale to a customer, discipline an employee without creating a backlash, conduct a staff meeting, or cajole a child into practicing his muscial instrument, we improve our chances of success by systematically considering how and where we will begin the discussion, the order in which we will discuss the topics, and the leverage we can use in trying to persuade someone to accept our proposal. In short, we apply the elements of BADGER. They are useful skills that enable us to cope with life's daily challenges.

As the diversity of examples in this book shows, however, assuming a mediator's role is an inescapable part of our lives. Whether we are formally appointed to serve in it or it is informally thrust upon us, we often manage the process of resolving conflict not by deciding how others must act but by prodding them—BADGERing them— into deciding for themselves how they will reconcile their differences. Being a capable mediator is not only important to individuals who want to do it vocationally; it is also invaluable to anyone else who wants to execute these tasks effectively.

Mediating well is not easy; it is a complex process with many variables. But this multiplicity of factors does not reduce mediating to an art form in which anything one does is acceptable or for which one must have an inborn talent. There are standards—the elements of BADGER—against which one can evaluate how well one is mediating. There are ways to prepare, duties to perform, and a structure to develop; there are options for trying to persuade parties to change their position and procedures for bringing discussions to a close. People can execute these responsibilities brilliantly or ineptly. They can also sharpen their skills in performing these tasks—they can become better at mediating.

Mediating is a rewarding role to play. It is more than just peacekeeping—restraining people from shooting at one another, literally or figuratively. While that is not an insignificant achievement, it is only the beginning. Cities do not become communities simply because there are no riots in the street. Corporations and universities do not become cohesive enterprises merely because colleagues are not operating at cross-purposes. They require a building process as well. A mediator can make a significant contribution to that process of building relationships among individuals, groups, or nations; he can help to structure arrangements that strengthen freedom and creativity, promote communication and trust, and secure dignity.

When people resolve their disputes, they feel not only relief, disappointment, or skepticism, but also an ineffable sense of exhilaration and pride. They have accomplished something; they have put something behind them and can get on with their lives. A mediator is not a bystander who merely observes such agreements develop. He is someone who commits his talents to managing a discussion process through which these disputants develop mutual commitments to action. He creates a climate that promotes reciprocal respect among the parties. He challenges parties to reach agreement by cooperating with, rather than prevailing over, each other. The final test of the value of their collective efforts comes when people must match their conduct to their rhetoric.

When the mediator knows he has contributed to the success of the process at each of these levels, the joy of mediating is unquenchable.

Selected Bibliography

Alfini, J., Press, S, Sternlight, J., and Stulberg, J. *Mediation Theory and Practice*. Newark, N.J.: Lexis Publishing, 2001.

Auerbach, J. *Justice Without Law?* New York: Oxford University Press, 1983.

Barry, B. *Theories of Justice*. Los Angeles: University of California Press, 1989.

_____. *Justice as Impartiality*. Oxford: Clarendon Press, 1995.

Brandt, R. *A Theory of the Good and the Right*. Oxford: Clarendon Press, 1979.

Bunker, B., and Rubin, J. and Associates. *Conflict, Cooperation, and Justice*. San Francisco: Jossey-Bass, 1995.

Bush, R., and Folger, J. *The Promise of Mediation*. San Francisco: Jossey-Bass, 1994.

Carpenter, S. and Kennedy, W.J.D. *Managing Public Disputes*. San Francisco: Jossey-Bass, 1988.

Costantino, C., and Merchant, C. *Designing Conflict Management Systems*. San Francisco: Jossey-Bass, 1996.

Coulson, R. *Professional Mediation of Civil Disputes*. New York: American Arbitration Association, 1984.

Deutsch, M. *The Resolution of Conflict*. New Haven: Yale University Press, 1973.

Dworkin, R. *Taking Rights Seriously*. Cambridge, Mass.: Belknap Press, 1978.

_____. *Law's Empire*. Cambridge, Mass.: Belknap Press, 1986.

_____. *Sovereign Virtue*. Cambridge, Mass.: Harvard University Press, 2000.

Elster, J. *The Cement of Society*. Cambridge: Cambridge University Press, 1989.

Elster, J. and Roemer, J. (eds.) *Interpersonal Comparisons of Well-Being*. Cambridge: Cambridge University Press, 1991.

Feinberg, J. *Rights, Justice, and the Bounds of Liberty*. Princeton: Princeton University Press, 1980.

_____. *Harm to Others*. New York: Oxford University Press, 1984.

Gilligan, C. *In a Different Voice*. Cambridge, Mass.: Harvard University Press, 1982.

Goldberg, S., Brett, J., and Ury, W. *Getting Disputes Resolved*. San Francisco: Jossey-Bass, 1988.

Goldberg, S.; Sander, F.; and Rogers, N. *Dispute Resolution* (3d ed.). New York: Aspen Law and Business, 1999.

Golann, D. *Mediating Legal Disputes*. New York: Aspen Law and Business, 1996.

Gutmann, A., and Thompson, D. *Democracy and Disagreement*. Cambridge, Mass.: The Belknap Press, 1996.

Hart, H.L.A. *The Concept of Law* (2d ed.). Oxford: Clarendon Press, 1994

Haynes, J. *The Fundamentals of Family Mediation*. Albany: State University of New York Press, (1994).

Kolb, D.M. *The Mediators*. Cambridge, Mass.: MIT Press, 1983.

_____ and Associates. *When Talk Works*. San Francisco: Jossey-Bass (1994).

Lax, D., and Sebenius, J. *The Manager as Negotiator*. New York: The Free Press, 1986.

Merry, S. *Getting Justice and Getting Even*. Chicago: The University of Chicago Press, 1990.

Nader, L. and Todd, H., eds. *The Dispute Process: Law in Ten Societies*. New York: Columbia University Press, 1978.

Nozick, R. *Anarchy, State and Utopia*. New York: Basic Books, 1974.

Rawls, J. *A Theory of Justice* (revised edition). Cambridge, Mass.: Belknap Press, 1999.

_____. *Political Liberalism*. New York: Columbia University Press. 1993.

Rubin, J., ed. *Dynamics of Third Party Intervention*. New York: Praeger, 1981.

Schelling, T. *The Strategy of Conflict*. Cambridge, Mass.: Harvard University Press, 1960.

Sen, A. *Collective Choice and Individual Values*. San Francisco: Holden-Day, 1970.

Susskind, L., and Cruikshank, J. *Breaking the Impasse*. New York: Basic Books, 1987.

Vroom, V.H., and Yetton, P.W. *Leadership and Decision Making*. Pittsburgh, Pa.: University of Pittsburgh Press, 1973.

Walton, R., and McKersie, R. *A Behavioral Theory of Labor Negotiations* (2nd edition). Ithaca, N.Y.: ILR Press, 1991.

Index

About the Author

Joseph B. Stulberg is Professor of Law at the Moritz College of Law at The Ohio State University and serves as Director of its nationally acclaimed comprehensive Program on Dispute Resolution. He earned his B.A. from Kalamazoo College, his J.D. from New York University School of Law, and his Ph.D. in philosophy from the University of Rochester. The first director of the Rochester Center for Dispute Settlement and a former Vice President of the American Arbitration Association, he is an active mediator and arbitrator of labor, commercial, construction, family and public policy disputes and has developed and conducted training programs for mediators in court-annexed programs, government agencies, and professional and community groups since 1973. He is a member of the New York Bar and such professional societies as the Association for Conflict Resolution and the Dispute Resolution Section of the American Bar Association. He has been a guest lecturer and visiting faculty member at various universities, including Cardozo Law School, Cornell University, Hamline University, Harvard Law School, New York University, and Pepperdine University School of Law; has taught seminars on conflict resolution and democratic theory at national universities in Hungary, Poland, and Romania; has appeared as a guest speaker and mediation trainer at numerous professional conferences; and has written extensively on the subject of conflict management.